To Desma
from Eleanor 1980

THE CARNIVAL GLASS COLLECTOR'S PRICE GUIDE

Merry Christmas

THE CARNIVAL GLASS COLLECTOR'S PRICE GUIDE

Marian Klamkin

Photographs by Charles Klamkin

HAWTHORN BOOKS

A Division of Elsevier-Dutton

New York

THE CARNIVAL GLASS COLLECTOR'S PRICE GUIDE

 All inquiries should be addressed to Elsevier-Dutton, 2 Park Avenue, New York, New York 10016. This book was manufactured in the United States of America and published simultaneously in Canada by Clarke, Irwin & Company Limited, Toronto and Vancouver.

Library of Congress Catalog Card Number: 77-92365

ISBN: 0-8015-1094-5

3 4 5 6 7 8 9 10

Introduction

This new, revised edition of *The Carnival Glass Collector's Price Guide* reflects more than the inflation-related rise in prices presently common to all American antiques and collectibles. The enthusiasm of the younger generation for the architecture and decorative art styles of the turn-of-the-century has led to competitive bidding in the salesrooms and at auction for the handsome iridescent glass known as "carnival." Within the past few years few important collections have been put up for sale. The glass, once cheap and abundant, is now scarce and desirable. Prices have risen for all pieces of carnival glass and especially for the rarities. This revision reflects a new wave of collectors, a tighter market, and the desirability of all American glass as collector's items.

Popularity in a single collecting category appears to come in waves. Around twenty years ago, the old iridescent glass made in America in the first quarter of this century began to attract the attention of collectors and within a five-year time span the glass, originally made to sell for pennies, became one of the most popular collecting categories in this country. Clubs were formed, books and price guides were written, patterns, colors, and shapes were identified, and research was begun on the four major manufacturers of canival glass.

Within a few years the demand for the rarest pieces of carnival glass was so great that prices rose accordingly. The status among collectors who owned such rarities as the large Millersburg pieces or certain pitcher and tumbler sets rose and antique dealers, seeing the booming market in carnival, began to specialize in this singular type of glass. Interest in carnival glass started in the Midwest but soon spread to both coasts as more and more glass collectors became fascinated with the great variety of colors, shapes, and patterns of this nostalgic-looking glass.

Unfortunately, those same early collectors of carnival glass were the people who wrote the price guides. They set the ever-increasing prices that soon got out of hand. Collecting went from an enjoyable hobby to a strongly competitive business and involved many "investors" rather than true collectors. Identification and price were the criteria for buying and a lot of trading went on at each club convention. Instead of appraising the glass as an artistic or historical accomplishment by American glassmakers, the only concern of many owners was the rapid rise in price and whether the prices would hold indefinitely.

It came as no surprise to those with experience in the antiques and collectibles market when, only a few years ago, the prices of carnival glass began to slide downward at a rather alarming rate. In addition, many of the early collectors were closing their family homes and retiring to smaller quarters and within a single year there were almost fifty major auctions of carnival glass. Younger collectors were able to buy rarities in carnival glass that they had never thought they would be able to own. Those older collectors who had been holding onto their collections read of the high prices brought at a few of the first auctions and arranged to sell their collections as well, and soon there was just too much carnival glass back on the market. A kind of panic set in and only a few collectors had enough faith to hold onto their collections and even to buy more as good pieces came on the market for the first time in a long time.

One of the reasons for the decline in carnival glass values was the encouragement by some early collectors for reproductions to be made—first as club convention souvenirs and, later, to make certain patterns in iridescent glass available to more people. The glass companies that were capable of producing respectable imitations of the old glass took advantage of the nostalgia wave of the 1960s and early 1970s by producing more and more iridescent glass. Most of this glass was clearly marked, but marks were later ground off and the pieces sold for "old" by unscrupulous dealers. Some people who understood the iridizing process bought old colored or clear glass and turned it into "carnival." There were so many reproductions and outright "fakes" that collectors had a difficult time keeping up with them, and there were few people among even the most experienced collectors who did not get stung at least once or twice.

Even though there was a valiant effort on the part of the editors of club newsletters to keep members informed on new iridescent glass, the market became too discouraging for many younger collectors to enter the collecting field. There was just too much to learn. There are almost 1,500 patterns, many shapes, a great variety of colors, and too many reproductions for carnival glass collecting to be easy. In addition, there is no real intrinsic value in the old glass. Yet, through all of this, there were some collectors who loved carnival glass and were able to take advantage of declining prices to add to their collections pieces they had never thought they would be able to afford.

The new wave of carnival glass collectors is quite different from the old. These younger people are fascinated by American glassmaking history. They realize that the glass hasn't too far to go before it is genuinely antique, but they are less interested in carnival as an investment potential than they are in its representation of a way of life that is gone and a kind of style in the decorative arts that is important. These collectors study the glassmaking history of this country and the various methods and materials used in producing the large quantities of glass with iridescent surfaces.

With the publication of *The Collector's Guide to Carnival Glass* in 1976, new collectors joined the clubs and began their collections from the auctions of the older pioneer collectors. There is no longer the same frenzy in buying and cooler heads prevail. Prices have once again begun to rise and, for the more heavily produced patterns and colors, the prices are now somewhat stable. It is now possible to write a more valid price guide than those previously written by dealers and collectors. The prices in the following pages were arrived at by averaging the prices paid most recently in various parts of the country. Carnival glass finally has become a more respectable collectible. If some of the older collector-dealers manipulated the market in such a way as to kill the goose that laid the iridescent egg, the new collectors will not repeat that error. They buy the glass to study it, to enjoy it, and to keep it. Many are more sensible and specialize in one company's glassware or in a single color or shape. The demand at present for known Millersburg glass is extremely high and will probably continue to climb.

More and more younger collectors have recently become fascinated with carnival glass and are participating in club activities in order to learn all they can about America's glass history. Glass collecting is a well-established hobby in this country and the carnival glass story is an important part of our business and social growth. The old-fashioned glass with shimmering surfaces fascinates more and more people as it comes closer to an age where it will be considered a true antique.

Colors in Carnival Glass

Iridescent glass was made in a variety of colors of base glass. In all cases, when discussing colors in carnival glass, collectors refer *only* to the base glass, that color you see when you hold the glass in front of a strong light. Almost every pattern and shape can be found in some shade of marigold. The deeper colors—green, blue, purple, and amethyst—are also found in numerous pieces of carnival. These colors will be found in a great variety of shades.

Pastel shades are less common and therefore usually more expensive. Within the past few years there have been many new collectors of the pastel opalescent shades and prices have risen for these relatively scarce pieces. Clambroth, a self-descriptive color, is in strong demand. The most desirable of all colors, however, is true red. Because red is a more expensive glass color to make, little of it was produced in carnival glass, since the manufacturers' intent was to sell the glass as cheaply as possible.

All colors in which carnival glass was made are illustrated in *The Collector's Guide to Carnival Glass* in the color insert between pages 22 and 23. In addition, close-up photographs of the more popular patterns and some rarities are illustrated in that book, to which this price guide is a companion.

It should be kept in mind that this price guide is *only* a guide. Some listed pieces will be found at much lower prices than those given here. The prices listed are retail prices and are generally higher than prices that will be paid at auction. Some prices may be slightly lower than those asked by reputable dealers. It is advisable that new collectors do business with dealers whom they trust and that they build their collections gradually and with caution. It is not difficult to detect new issues made from the old glass once a collector has become experienced. As many collectors who have already read *The Collector's Guide to Carnival Glass* know, specialized collections are always worth more, and complete sets such as table sets, water sets, or punch sets are always in greater demand than the individual pieces.

All prices quoted herein are for perfect pieces only. Bubbles in the glass, mold marks, and other intrinsic imperfections are indigenous to carnival glass and do not detract from its value. Chips and cracks, however, do devalue the glass, and collectors should examine each piece carefully before purchase.

There have been a few "discoveries" in the past years concerning some pieces that are high priced and always in demand by advanced collectors. The small bottle called the Buzz Saw Cruet by collectors, was made in two sizes and is, in reality, a cologne or dresser bottle. The Venetian Rose Bowl was also advertised as a lamp base in an old Butler's Catalog. The completed lamp had a large matching glass shade.

There are still many bargains to be found in carnival glass and pieces are still stored in attics and basements that have yet to be recorded and put up for sale. There is always the chance that important pieces of carnival glass will turn up at garage sales and flea markets at very low prices. The chances for finding bargains become fewer, but the possibility is always there.

Iridescence

All collectors of carnival glass are aware that the quality of iridescence will vary from piece to piece and from manufacturer to manufacturer. Perhaps the finest iridescence was developed by the Millersburg Company and that, plus the limited output of this short-lived firm, is why Millersburg has become the "cream" of carnival collections. One can expect prices for Millersburg pieces to rise more rapidly than those of most other iridescent glass. As an investment, Millersburg pieces have become extremely desirable.

Quality of iridescence will dictate price to a certain extent. Collectors search for the best examples of overall high iridescence in all carnival glass.

Pattern	Marigold	Green, Blue, Amethyst, Purple	Pastel	Red
ACANTHUS				
Bowl, 7"-9"	$ 60.00	$100.00		
Compote	45.00	75.00		
Hat shape	32.50	55.00		
Plate, 9"	125.00	175.00	$145.00 (clambroth)	

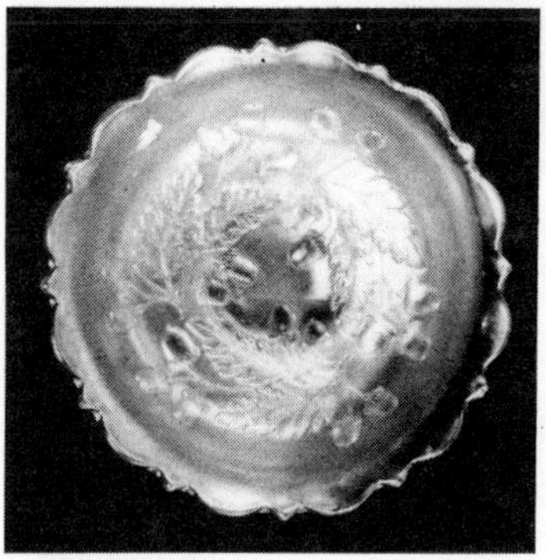

Pattern	Marigold	Green, Blue, Amethyst, Purple	Pastel	Red
ACORN				
Bowl, 7"-9"	$30.00	$ 50.00		
Plate, 9"		345.00		
ACORN BURR				
Berry bowl, 9", 10"	$125.00	$155.00	$ 300.00	
Berry bowl (indiv.), 5"	25.00	45.00	80.00	
Butter dish with cover	200.00	300.00	500.00	
Creamer	75.00	125.00	200.00	
Spooner	75.00	125.00	200.00	
Sugar bowl	100.00	150.00	210.00	
Punch bowl with stand	400.00	600.00	1,125.00	
Punch cup	45.00	60.00	100.00	
Tumbler	50.00	70.00	100.00	
AGE HERALD				
Bowl, 9"		$ 950.00		
Plate		1,125.00		
AMARYLLIS				
Compote	$40.00	$50.00		

Pattern	Marigold	Green, Blue, Amethyst, Purple	Pastel	Red

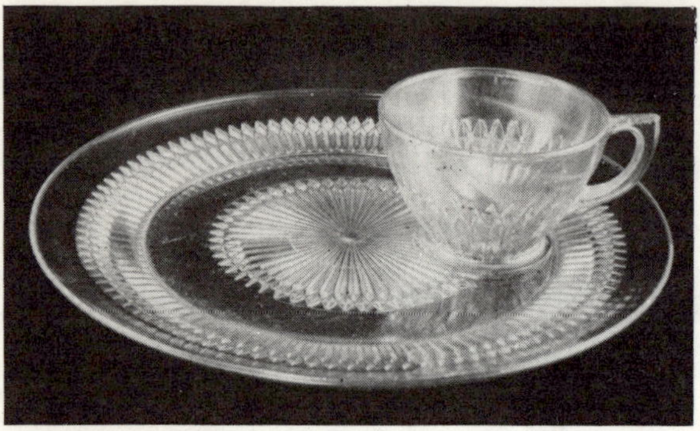

ANNIVERSARY (late pattern)

Snack set (plate and cup)	$15.00			

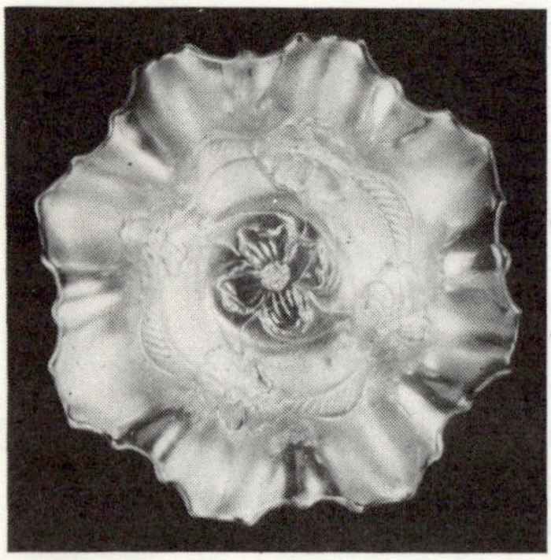

APPLE BLOSSOMS				
Bowl	$ 35.00	$ 45.00	$ 75.00	
Compote	40.00	50.00	125.00	
Candy dish	30.00	42.50		
APPLE BLOSSOM TWIGS				
Bowl, 9"	$ 40.00	$ 55.00	$ 75.00	
Plate, 9"	80.00	100.00	145.00 (peach opalescent)	
APPLE PANELS				
Creamer	$ 30.00	$ 52.50		
Sugar Bowl	40.00	60.00		
APPLE TREE				
Pitcher	$125.00	$250.00	$400.00	
Tumbler	30.00	50.00	87.50	

Pattern	Marigold	Green, Blue, Amethyst, Purple	Pastel	Red
APRIL SHOWERS				
Vase, 11"-12"		$80.00		
ARCADIA BASKETS				
Plate, 8"	$35.00			
ARCS (IMPERIAL)				
Bowl	$35.00	$50.00	$62.50	
Compote	25.00	35.00	50.00	
ASTERS				
Bowl	$27.50			
AUGUST FLOWER				
Bowl	$25.00			
AURORA				
Bowl, 8"-9"		$60.00	$137.50 (ice white)	
AUSTRALIAN SWAN				
Bowl, 5½"	$115.00	$170.00		

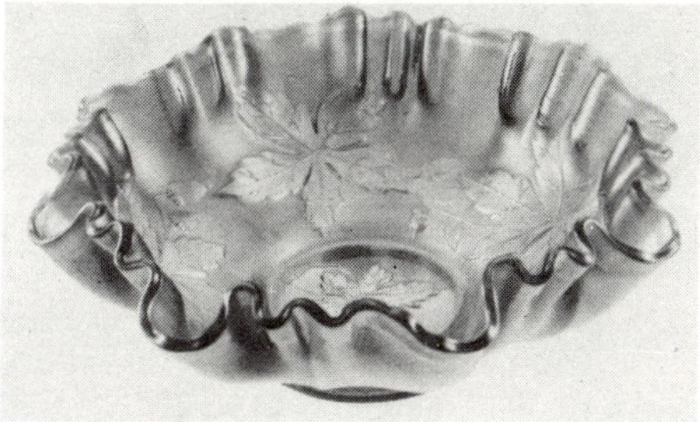

Pattern	Marigold	Green, Blue, Amethyst, Purple	Pastel	Red
AUTUMN ACORNS				
Bowl, 7"-9"	$50.00	$75.00	$100.00	$325.00
Plate, 8"-9"	62.50	80.00	100.00	
AZTEC				
Creamer	$40.00			
Sugar bowl	45.00			
BALLOONS				
Cake plate with handles		$75.00	$100.00	
Compote		50.00		

Pattern	*Marigold*	*Green, Blue, Amethyst, Purple*	*Pastel*	*Red*
BAMBOO BIRD				
Pickle castor jar, 6 1/8"		$280.00		
BANDED DIAMONDS				
Pitcher	$175.00	$300.00		
Tumbler	40.00	50.00		
BANDED DRAPE				
Pitcher	$150.00	$250.00	$350.00	
Tumbler	30.00	45.00	62.50	
BASKET (NORTHWOOD)	$75.00	$125.00	$150.00 (ice green)	
			127.50 (ice blue)	
			210.00 (aqua opalescent)	
BASKETWEAVE				
Hat whimsey	$45.00	$140.00		$250.00
BASKETWEAVE AND CABLE				
Creamer	$30.00			
Sugar bowl	35.00			
BEADED BASKET	$35.00	$55.00	$75.00	
BEADED BULL'S EYE				
Vases (pulled out, various sizes)	$30.00	$40.00	$ 55.00	
	60.00	85.00	125.00	
BEADED CABLE				
Candy dish	$40.00	$60.00	$100.00	
Rose bowl	75.00	95.00	150.00 (aqua opalescent)	
BEADED HEARTS				
Bowl	$50.00	$65.00		
BEADED SHELL				
Berry bowl, footed, 9"	$ 70.00	$110.00		
Berry bowl, footed, 5"	30.00	70.00		
Butter dish with cover	150.00	275.00		

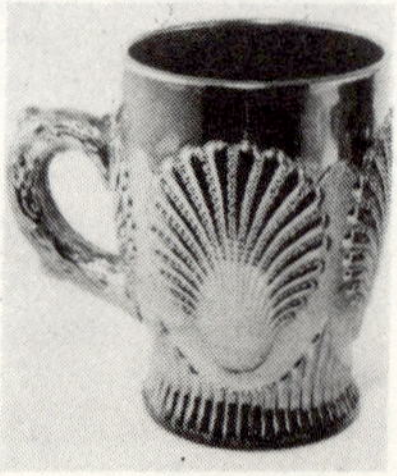

Pattern	Marigold	Green, Blue, Amethyst, Purple	Pastel	Red
Creamer	$ 55.00	$ 95.00		
Sugar bowl	70.00	100.00		
Spooner	55.00	90.00		
Mug	140.00	125.00		
Pitcher	325.00	450.00		
BERNHEIMER BOWL		$250.00 (blue) 350.00 (amethyst)		
BERRY BASKET	$60.00			
BIG BASKETWEAVE				
Basket	$60.00	$75.00	$90.00	
Vase	30.00	40.00	55.00	
BIG FISH (TROUT AND FLY) (MILLERSBURG)				
Bowl	$200.00	$250.00		
Plate		500.00		
BIRD AND CHERRIES				
Bonbon with handles	$45.00	$ 55.00		
Bowl		225.00		
Compote	50.00	55.00		
Mug	60.00	85.00		
Plate		950.00		
BIRD WITH GRAPES				
Wall pocket (vase)	$150.00	$190.00		
BIRMINGHAM AGE HERALD (See AGE HERALD)				
BLACKBERRY				
Bowl, 9"	$30.00	$40.00		
Compote	25.00	40.00		
Compote, small	40.00	55.00		
Hat	20.00	30.00		

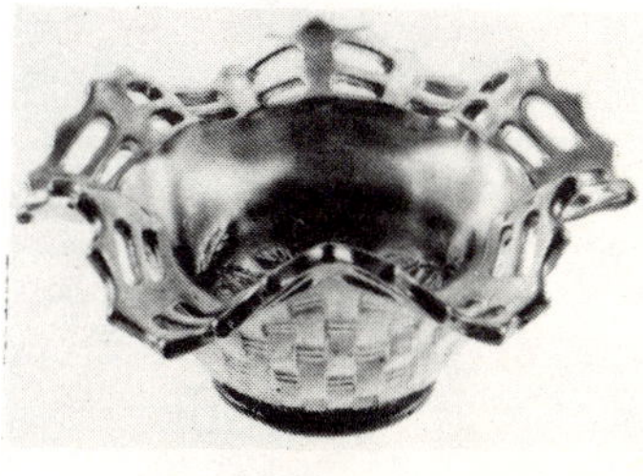

$200.00

Pattern	Marigold	Green, Blue, Amethyst, Purple	Pastel	Red
BLACKBERRY BLOCK				
Pitcher	$200.00	$250.00	$525.00 (clambroth)	
Tumbler	40.00	60.00	100.00 (clambroth)	

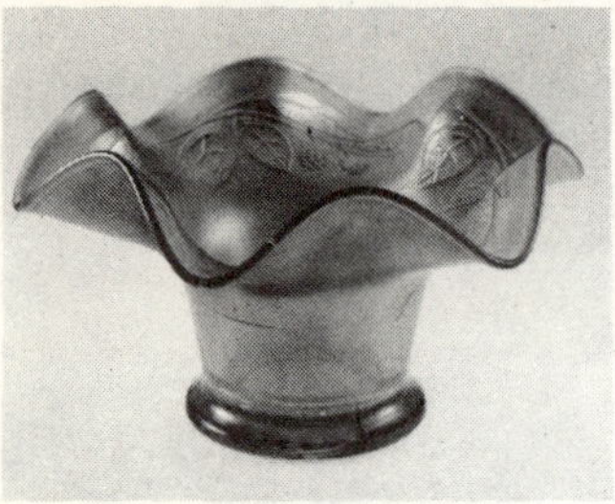

Pattern	Marigold	Green, Blue, Amethyst, Purple	Pastel	Red
BLACKBERRY SPRAY				
Hat	$25.00	$35.00		
BLACKBERRY WREATH				
Bowl, 8"	$55.00	$125.00		
Bowl, 5"	30.00	40.00		
Epergne		275.00		
Gravy or sauce boat			$90.00	
BLOSSOM AND BAND				
Berry bowl, 9"	$ 30.00			
Berry bowl, 5"	15.00			
Bud vase (automobile)	25.00	$ 50.00		
Lamp	250.00	275.00		
BLOSSOMS AND SPEARS				
Plate	$20.00			
BLUEBERRY				
Pitcher	$325.00	$425.00	$500.00	
Tumbler	45.00	60.00	100.00	
BO-PEEP CHILD'S SET				
Bowl	$40.00	$50.00		
Mug	40.00	50.00		
BOUQUET				
Pitcher	$160.00	$300.00		
Tumbler	45.00	60.00		

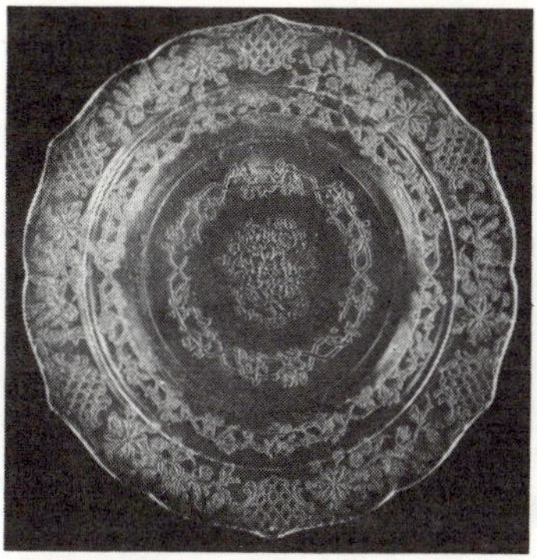

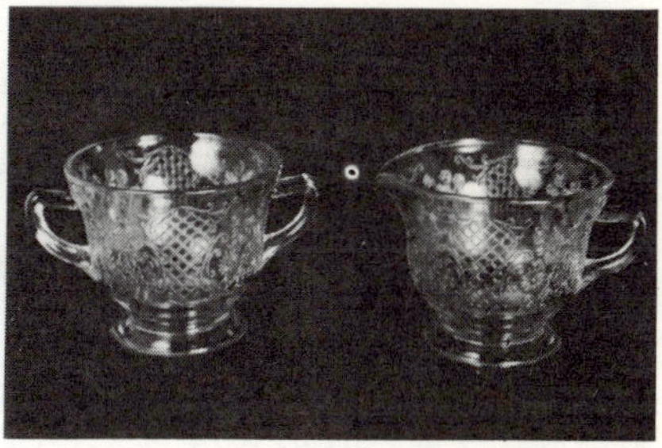

Pattern	Marigold	Green, Blue, Amethyst, Purple	Pastel	Red
BOUQUET AND LATTICE (also called NORMANDIE)				
Plate, 10½"	$7.50			
Grille plate	5.50			
Plate, 9¼"	5.00			
Plate, 8"	5.00			
Plate, 6"	3.50			
Bowl, 5"	2.50			
Cup	7.00			
Saucer	3.50			
Creamer	7.50			
Sugar bowl	7.50			
BROCADED ACORNS				
Bonbon			$50.00	
Bread tray			50.00	
Cake plate			65.00	
BROKEN ARCHES				
Punch bowl	$200.00	$550.00		
Punch cup	20.00	32.50		
BROOKFIELD				
Deviled egg plate		$80.00		
BROOKLYN BRIDGE				
Bowl	$350.00			

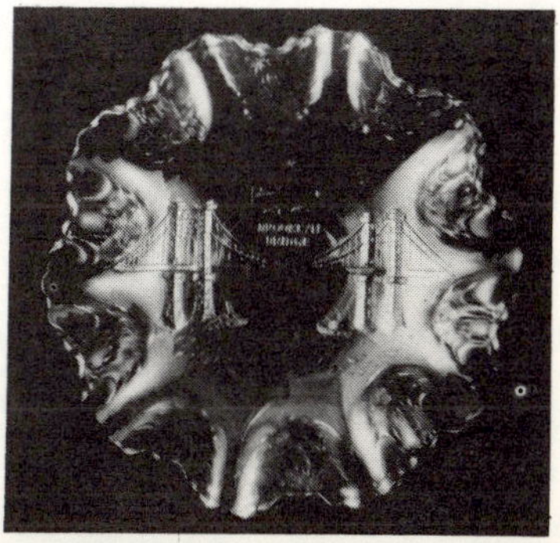

Pattern	Marigold	Green, Blue, Amethyst, Purple	Pastel	Red
BUTTERFLIES				
Bonbon	$30.00	$42.50		

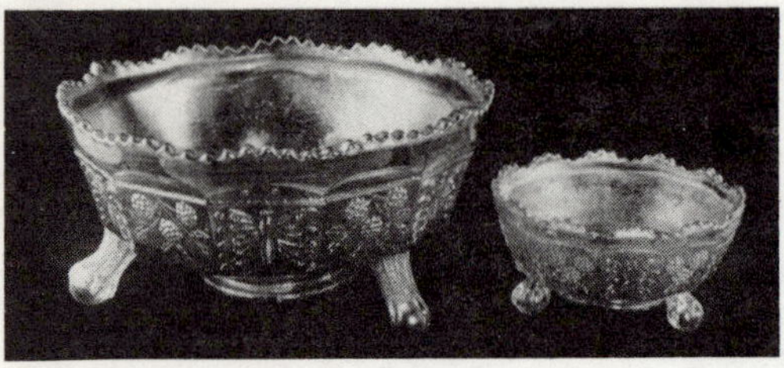

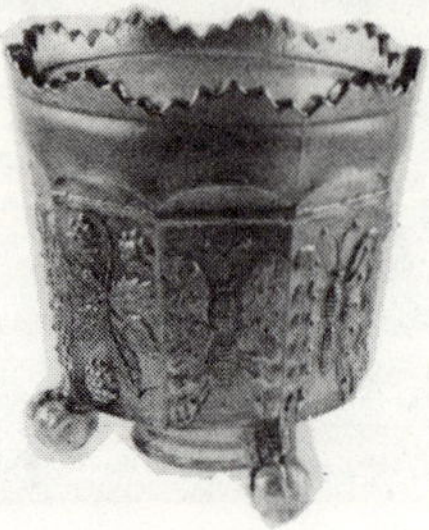

Pattern	Marigold	Green, Blue, Amethyst, Purple	Pastel	Red
BUTTERFLY AND BERRY				
Bowl, footed, 9"	$ 45.00	$ 70.00		
Bowl, footed, 5"	22.50	30.00		
Butter dish with cover	125.00	180.00		
Creamer	40.00	60.00		
Sugar bowl	50.00	75.00		
Spooner	40.00	62.50		
Cuspidor	500.00	625.00		
Hatpin holder	200.00	500.00		
Pitcher	125.00	250.00		
Tumbler	30.00	50.00		
Vase	30.00	50.00		$170.00
Hatpin holder whimsey	650.00	700.00		
BUTTERFLY AND FERN				
Pitcher	$200.00	$500.00		
Tumbler	40.00	55.00		
BUTTERFLY AND TULIP				
Bowl, footed	$ 250.00	$ 700.00		
Bowl, shallow, square	1,000.00	1,750.00		
BUTTERFLY BUSH				
Open compote, large	$125.00	$200.00		
BUZZ SAW				
Cruet, 4"	$450.00	$500.00		
Cruet, 6"	425.00	550.00		

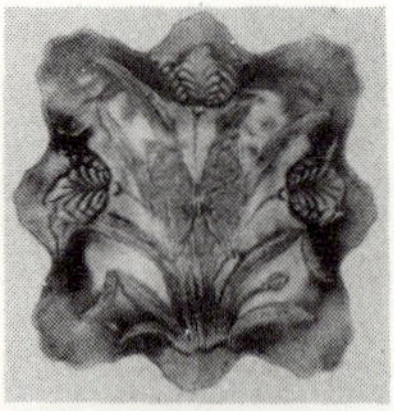

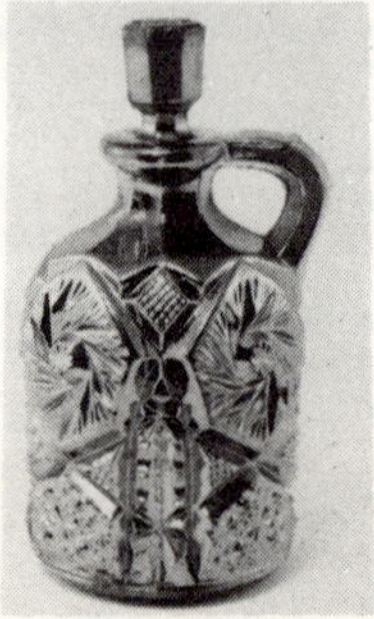

Pattern	Marigold	Green, Blue, Amethyst, Purple	Pastel	Red
CACTUS				
Bowl, 9"	$25.00	$60.00		
CANE				
Bowl, 10"	$30.00			
Pickle or relish dish	35.00			
Wineglass	45.00			
CAPTIVE ROSE				
Bowl, 10"	$35.00	$ 40.00		
Compote	35.00	40.00		
Bonbon with handles	35.00	40.00		
Plate, 9"	80.00	125.00		
Plate, 6"	35.00	45.00		
CARNIVAL HOBSTAR				
Bowl, 12"	$ 35.00			
Bowl, 5"	15.00			
Butter dish with cover	90.00	$170.00		
Creamer	35.00	85.00		
Sugar bowl with lid	50.00	100.00		
Spooner	35.00	95.00		
Cracker jar	60.00			
Pickle castor	350.00			
CARNIVAL HOLLY				
Bowl, 9"	$40.00	$70.00		$350.00
Compote	40.00	70.00		
Hat	30.00	40.00		400.00

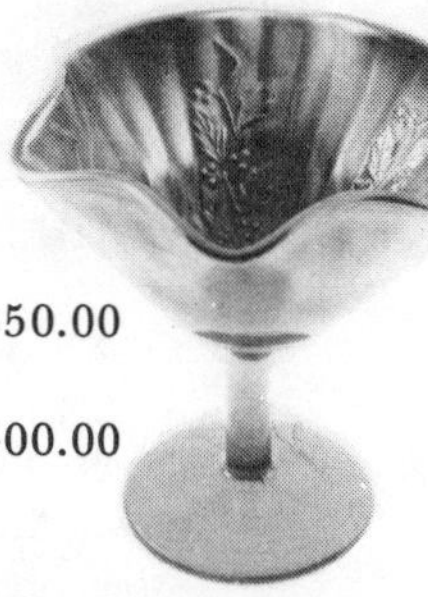

Pattern	Marigold	Green, Blue, Amethyst, Purple	Pastel	Red
CARNIVAL THISTLE				
Bowl, 9"	$ 40.00	$ 55.00		
Compote	30.00	40.00		
Plate, 9"	150.00	225.00		

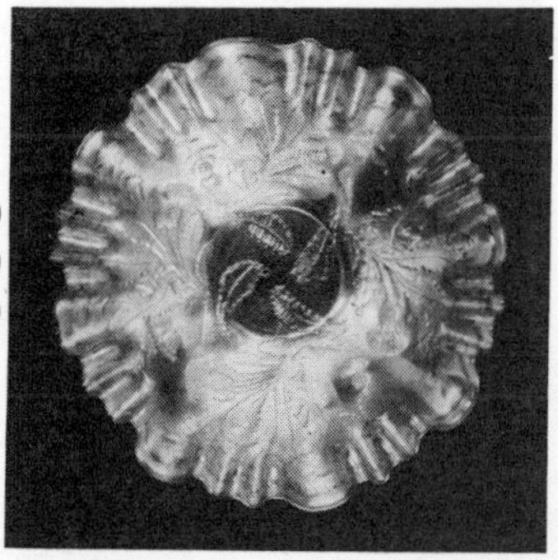

Pattern	Marigold	Green, Blue, Amethyst, Purple	Pastel	Red
CAROLINA DOGWOOD				
Bowl, 9"	$30.00	$42.50	$100.00 (peach opalescent)	
CAROLINE				
Bowl, 9"	$40.00		$ 75.00 (peach opalescent)	
Bride's basket			100.00 (peach opalescent)	
Applied-handle basket			150.00 (peach opalescent)	

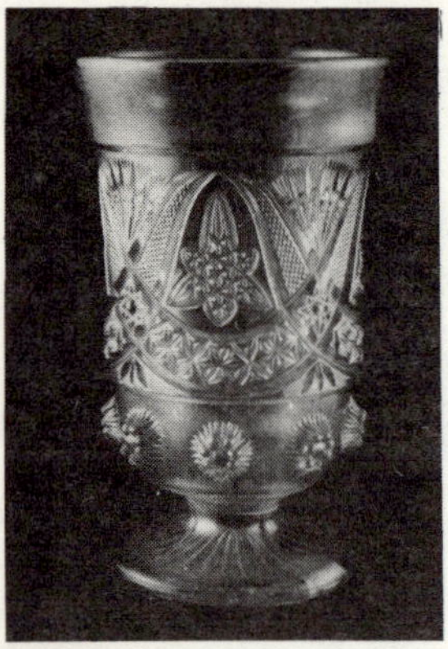

CATHEDRAL CHALICE	$150.00	$250.00		
CATTAILS AND WATER LILIES				
Bowl, 9"	$ 40.00	$ 50.00		
Bowl, 5"	25.00	35.00		
Bowl, oval, footed	100.00	145.00		
Butterdish with cover	125.00	150.00		
Creamer	50.00	200.00		
Sugar bowl	60.00	200.00		
Spooner	55.00	200.00		
Pitcher	100.00	200.00		
Tumbler	25.00	45.00		
Toothpick holder	50.00			
CHATELAINE				
Pitcher		$1,750.00		
Tumbler		225.00		

Pattern	Marigold	Green, Blue, Amethyst, Purple	Pastel	Red
CHECKERBOARD				
Goblet		$ 250.00		
Pitcher		2,000.00		
Tumbler		225.00		
CHERRY CHAIN				
Bonbon	$25.00	$ 35.00	$50.00	
Bowl, 9"	40.00	55.00	75.00	
CHERRY (FENTON)				
Bonbon with handles	$25.00	$ 35.00		
Bowl	45.00	62.50		
Plate	75.00	125.00		
CHERRY (MILLERSBURG)				
Butterdish with cover	$150.00	$175.00		
Creamer	40.00	65.00		
Sugar bowl with cover	50.00	75.00		
Spooner	40.00	60.00		
Milk pitcher	200.00	375.00		
Pitcher	250.00	400.00		
Tumbler	80.00	100.00		
CHERRY (NORTHWOOD)				
Bowl, 9"	$40.00	$50.00	$75.00	

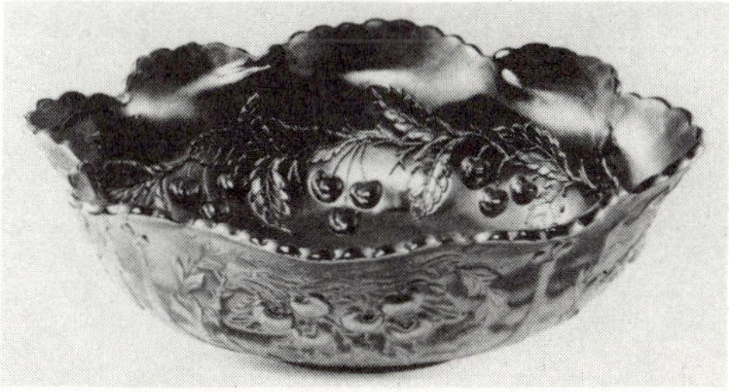

Pattern	Marigold	Green, Blue, Amethyst, Purple	Pastel	Red
CHERRY WREATH				
Berry bowl, oval	$100.00	$125.00	$200.00	
Berry bowl (indiv.), oval	30.00	40.00	65.00	
Pitcher	150.00	200.00	500.00	
Tumbler	45.00	65.00	110.00	

Pattern	Marigold	Green, Blue, Amethyst, Purple	Pastel	Red
CHRISTMAS COMPOTE	$2,500.00	$3,000.00		
CHRYSANTHEMUM				
Bowl, 11"	$50.00	$75.00		$500.00
CIRCLED SCROLL				
Bowl	$ 30.00	$ 45.00		
Creamer	35.00	45.00		
Sugar bowl	40.00	50.00		
Pitcher	125.00	175.00		
Tumbler	30.00	45.00		
Vase	45.00	70.00		
CLEVELAND MEMORIAL TRAY	$2,000.00	$1,750.00		

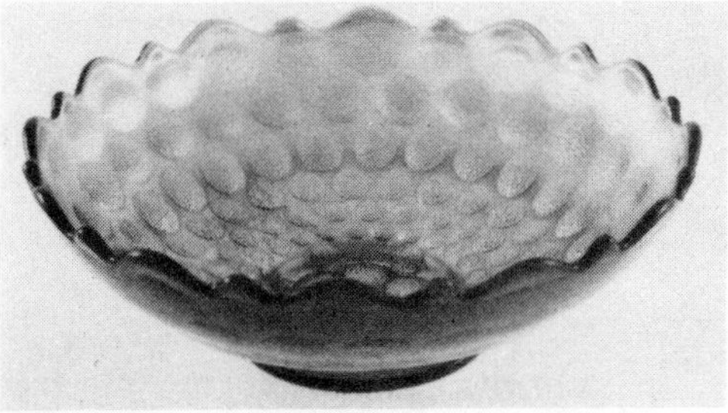

Pattern	Marigold	Green, Blue, Amethyst, Purple	Pastel	Red
COIN DOT				
Bowl, 9"	$ 35.00	$ 45.00		$350.00
Pitcher	200.00	500.00		
Plate, 9"		150.00		
Rose bowl	50.00	60.00		
Tumbler	50.00	75.00		
COIN SPOT				
Basket	$50.00	$70.00		
Bowl	40.00	50.00		
Compote	30.00	55.00	$75.00	
COLONIAL				
Bowl	$55.00			
Candlesticks	35.00			
Toothpick holder	65.00	$100.00		
Vase	35.00	75.00		

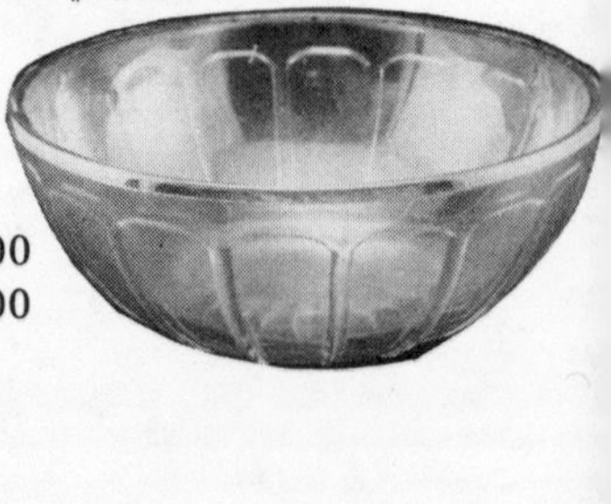

Pattern	Marigold	Green, Blue, Amethyst, Purple	Pastel	Red
COMET				
Bowl, 9"	$40.00	$ 60.00		
Plate, 9"	75.00	115.00		
CONCAVE DIAMONDS				
Castor jar	$250.00			
Pitcher			$400.00 (ice blue)	
Tumbler			100.00 (ice blue)	
CONCAVE FLUTE				
Rose bowl		$100.00		
CONCORD GRAPE				
Bowl	$ 45.00	$ 60.00		
Plate	350.00	550.00		
CORAL				
Bowl, 9"	$ 45.00	$ 60.00		
Compote	35.00	45.00		
Plate	325.00	550.00		
CORINTH				
Banana dish	$40.00	$ 50.00		
Bowl, 9"	40.00	45.00		
Vase	30.00	35.00		
Plate, 10"	90.00	140.00		
CORN				
Bottle, 5"	$225.00	$300.00	$325.00 (smoke)	
Vase	475.00	325.00	1,250.00 (ice blue)	
CORNUCOPIA				
Candlestick	$35.00		$55.00	
Vase	42.50		75.00	

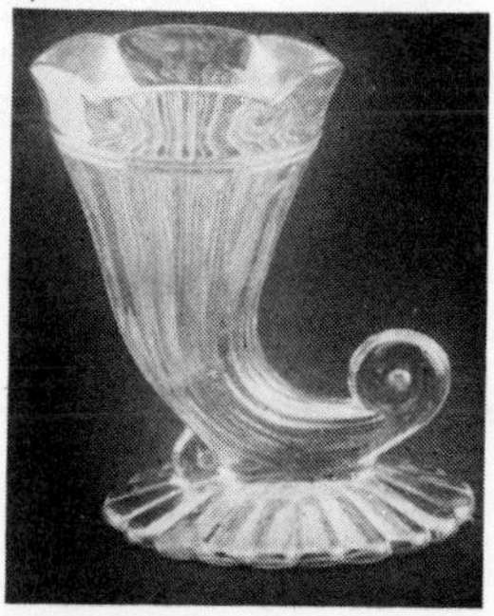

Pattern	Marigold	Green, Blue, Amethyst, Purple	Pastel	Red
COSMOS				
Bowl, 9"-10½"	$40.00	$ 75.00		
Compote	30.00	40.00		
Plate	75.00	50.00		
Plate, 9"-10"		100.00		

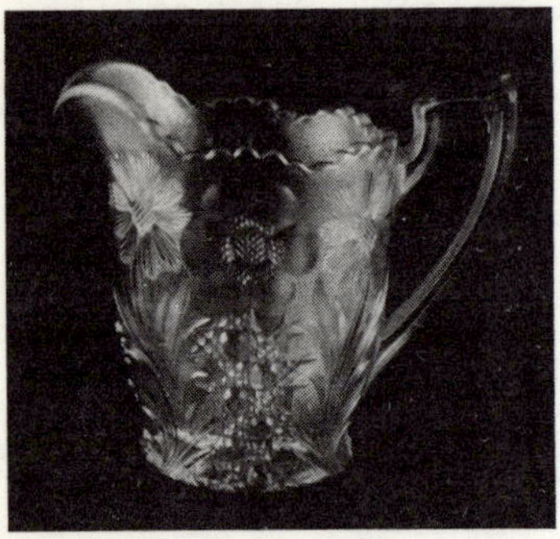

Pattern	Marigold	Green, Blue, Amethyst, Purple	Pastel	Red
COSMOS AND CANE				
Butterdish with cover	$150.00	$225.00	$150.00 (white, clambroth)	
Creamer	60.00	95.00	100.00	
Sugar bowl with cover	75.00	95.00	110.00	
Spooner	60.00	100.00	100.00	
Pitcher	150.00	210.00	500.00	
Tumbler	40.00	70.00	100.00	
Bowl, 9"	30.00	40.00	100.00	
Bowl, 5"	20.00	30.00	65.00	
COUNTRY KITCHEN				
Butter dish with cover	$160.00	$ 260.00		
Sugar bowl with cover	75.00	110.00		
Creamer	65.00	100.00		
Cuspidor		3,000.00		
Spooner	65.00	100.00		
COURTHOUSE PLATE (MILLERSBURG)				
Lettered plate		$350.00		
Unlettered, ruffled edge		650.00		

Pattern	Marigold	Green, Blue, Amethyst, Purple	Pastel	Red
CRAB CLAW				
Berry bowl, 9"	$ 40.00	$100.00		
Berry bowl, 5"	25.00	35.00		
Pitcher	300.00	500.00		
Tumbler	45.00	75.00		
CRACKLE				
Bowl, 9"	30.00	$ 50.00		
Bowl, 5"	15.00	20.00		
Bud vase (for automobile)	17.50	40.00		
Punch bowl with base	75.00	100.00		
Punch cup	15.00	20.00		
Pitcher	55.00	175.00		
Tumbler	15.00	50.00		
CURVED STAR				
Bowl, 9"	$ 35.00	$50.00		
Candlestick	50.00			
Epergne	225.00			
Flower vase	125.00			
CUT ARCS				
Bowl, 9"	$35.00	$50.00		
Compote	25.00	45.00		
CUT COSMOS				
Pitcher	$200.00	$450.00		
Tumbler	65.00	110.00		
DAHLIA				
Berry bowl, 9"	$ 65.00	$125.00	$150.00	
Berry bowl, 5"	25.00	50.00	75.00	
Butter dish with cover	200.00	250.00	300.00	
Creamer	60.00	100.00	125.00	
Sugar bowl with cover	65.00	110.00	135.00	
Spooner	60.00	100.00	125.00	
Pitcher	250.00	500.00	600.00	
Tumbler	50.00	100.00	110.00	
DAISIES AND DRAPES				
Vase	$100.00	$100.00	$125.00	
DAISY (FENTON)				
Bonbon	$35.00	$45.00		

Pattern	Marigold	*Green, Blue, Amethyst, Purple*	Pastel	Red

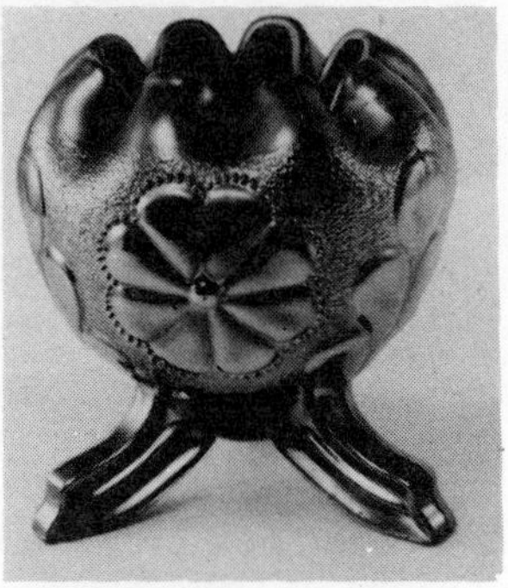

Pattern	Marigold	Green, Blue, Amethyst, Purple	Pastel	Red
DAISY AND PLUME				
Candy dish, footed	$30.00	$50.00	$100.00	
Compote	30.00	50.00	100.00	
Rose bowl, footed	50.00	75.00	125.00	
DAISY WREATH				
Bowl, 9"	$40.00			
DANDELION (NORTHWOOD)				
Mug	$100.00	$125.00	$400.00 (aqua opalescent)	
Pitcher	250.00	600.00	650.00	
Tumbler	50.00	100.00	145.00	
DANDELION PANELED				
Pitcher	$250.00	$350.00	$400.00	
Tumbler	50.00	75.00	95.00	

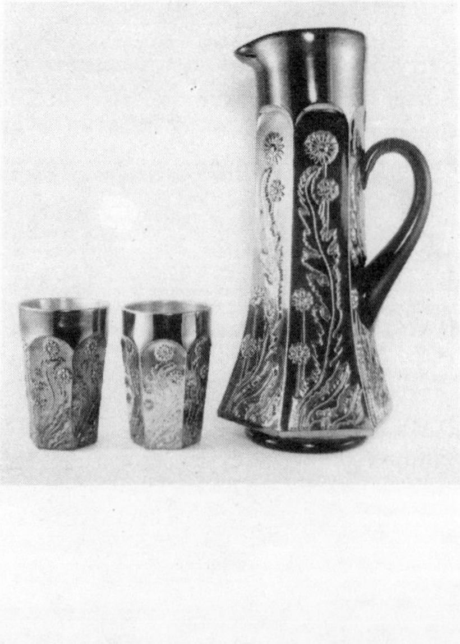

Pattern	Marigold	Green, Blue, Amethyst, Purple	Pastel	Red
DAVIDSON CHOCOLATES				
(Advertising plate)	$200.00	$250.00		
DIAMOND AND FILE				
Bowl	$25.00			
DIAMOND AND RIB				
Vase	$25.00	$45.00		
DIAMOND AND SUNBURST				
Bowl	$35.00	$ 45.00		
Wine decanter	60.00	300.00		
Wineglass	25.00	75.00		
DIAMOND AND THUMBPRINT				
Pitcher	$140.00	$200.00		
Tumbler	50.00	75.00		
DIAMOND LACE				
Berry bowl, 9"	$ 35.00	$100.00		
Berry bowl, 5"	17.50	30.00		
Fruit bowl	50.00	100.00		
Pitcher	150.00	300.00		
Tumbler	35.00	70.00		
DIAMOND POINT COLUMNS				
Compote	$25.00			
Butter dish with cover	85.00			
Creamer	40.00			
Sugar bowl with lid	45.00			
Spooner	40.00			
Plate, 7"	35.00			
Vase	45.00			
DIAMOND RING				
Bowl, 9"	$30.00		$70.00	
Bowl, 5"	15.00		25.00	
Fruit bowl	35.00	$50.00	70.00	

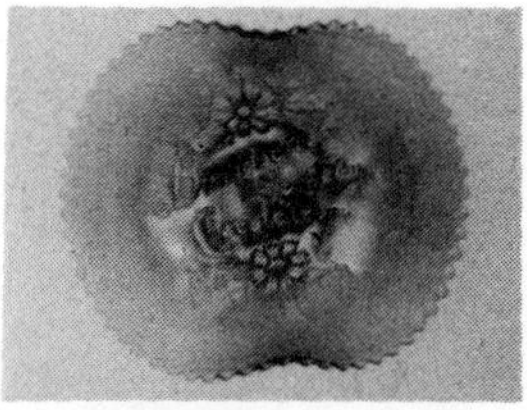

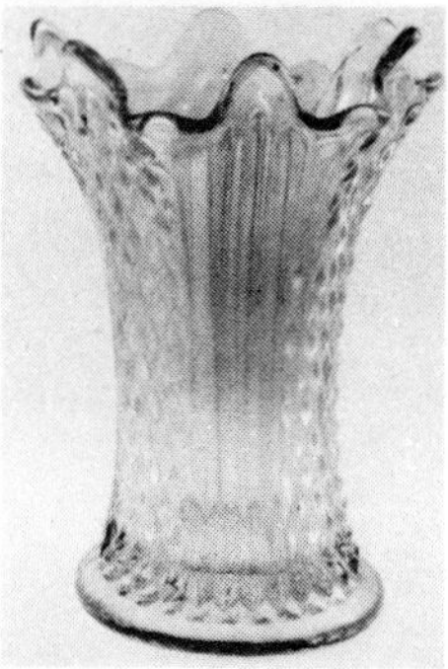

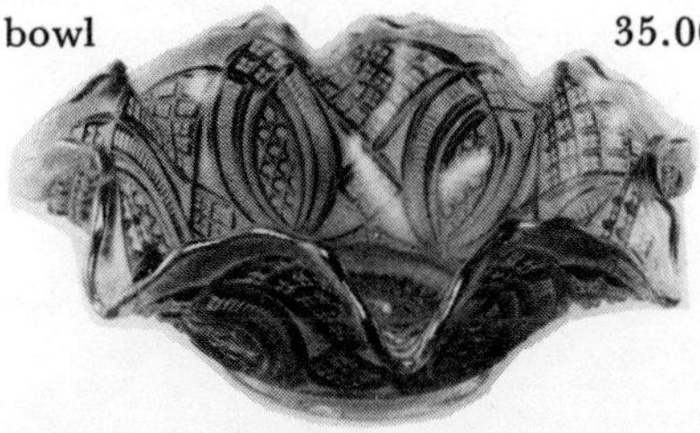

Pattern	Marigold	Green, Blue, Amethyst, Purple	Pastel	Red
DIVIDING DOLPHINS				
Bowl, footed	$150.00	$250.00		
DOGWOOD SPRAYS				
Banana bowl, footed		$125.00	$150.00	
Bowl, 9"		50.00		
Compote	$30.00	40.00		
DOLPHINS				
Compote	$475.00	$600.00		
DOUBLE DOLPHIN				
Bowl, footed 9"		$100.00	$125.00	
Cake plate with handles		50.00	65.00	
Candlesticks			60.00	
Compote			75.00	
Vase			80.00	

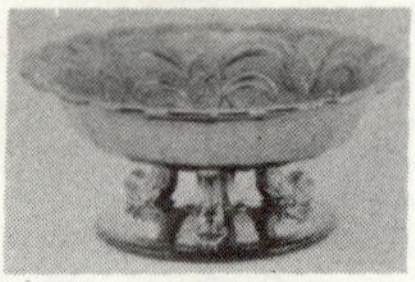

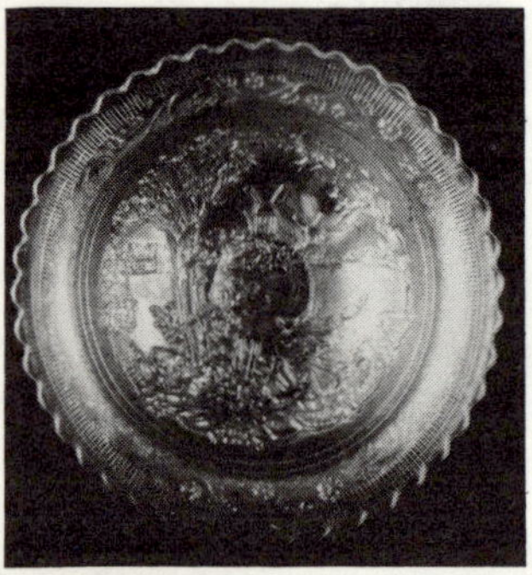

Pattern	Marigold	Green, Blue, Amethyst, Purple	Pastel	Red
DOUBLE DUTCH				
Bowl, footed, 9"	$35.00	$100.00		
DOUBLE SCROLL				
Bowl, oval	$30.00	$40.00	$55.00	
Candlesticks	30.00	40.00	75.00	
Punch cup	15.00			
DOUBLE STAR				
Pitcher	$200.00	$350.00		
Tumbler	60.00	75.00		
DOUBLE STEM ROSE				
Bowl	$40.00	$60.00	$100.00	

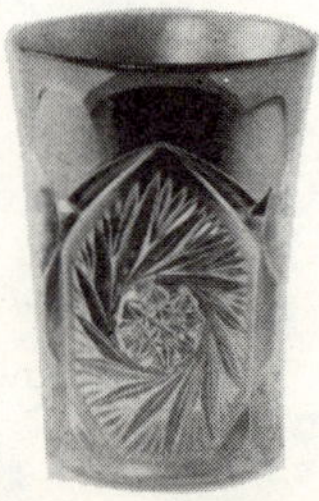

Pattern	Marigold	Green, Blue, Amethyst, Purple	Pastel	Red

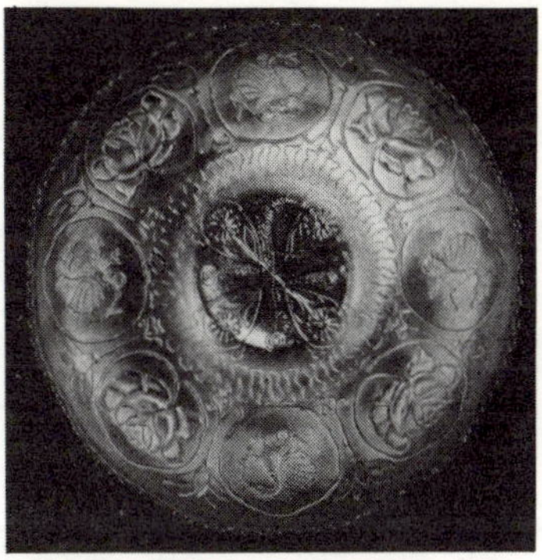

DRAGON AND LOTUS				
Bowl, 9"	$ 40.00	$ 45.00	$ 85.00	$400.00
Bowl, footed	45.00	70.00	100.00	450.00
Plate	200.00	300.00	500.00	825.00
DRAGON AND STRAWBERRY				
Bowl	$150.00	$300.00		

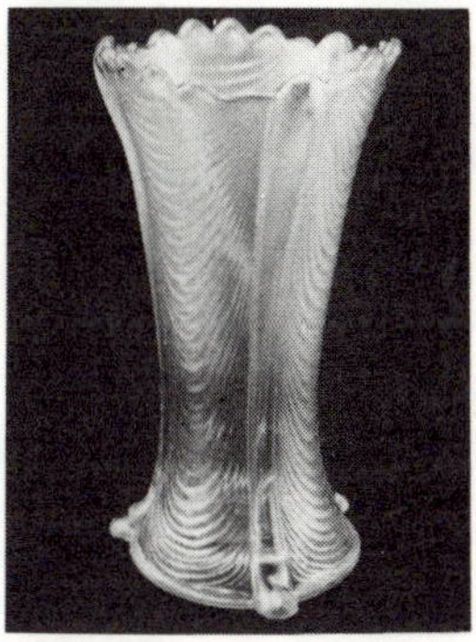

DRAPE				
Candy dish, footed	$40.00		$75.00 (ice blue)	
Vase	50.00		75.00	
DRAPERY (NORTHWOOD)				
Candy dish	$35.00	$ 45.00	$ 60.00	
Pitcher			525.00	
Tumbler			100.00	
Rose bowl	65.00	100.00	200.00 (aqua opalescent)	

Pattern	Marigold	Green, Blue, Amethyst, Purple	Pastel	Red
DUTCH PLATE	$30.00			
ELK (one-eyed)(FENTON)				
Bowl		$400.00		
Plate		650.00		
ELK (two-eyed) (MILLERSBURG)				
Bowl		$ 600.00		
Plate		825.00		
Paperweight		1,000.00		
EMBROIDERED MUMS				
Bonbon			$150.00	
Bowl, 9"	$60.00	$100.00	125.00	
Plate	60.00	95.00	125.00	
EMU				
Bowl, 10"	$150.00	$175.00		
ENGRAVED GRAPE				
Pitcher	$225.00			
Tumbler	75.00			
Tumbler, small	50.00			
ESTATE				
Creamer			$35.00	
Sugar bowl			42.50	
Perfume bottle		$125.00		
EXCHANGE BANK				
Plate		$300.00		
FAN				
Sauceboat	$125.00	$200.00		
Vase	35.00	45.00	$55.00	
FANCIFUL				
Bowl, 9"	$40.00	$ 55.00	$100.00	
Plate	90.00	100.00	175.00	
FANCY CUT				
Creamer	$50.00			

Pattern	Marigold	*Green, Blue, Amethyst, Purple*	Pastel	Red
FANCY FLOWERS				
Compote	$60.00	$100.00		
FARMYARD BOWL				
Round		$2,250.00		
Square		2,750.00 7,500.00 (green; one known)		

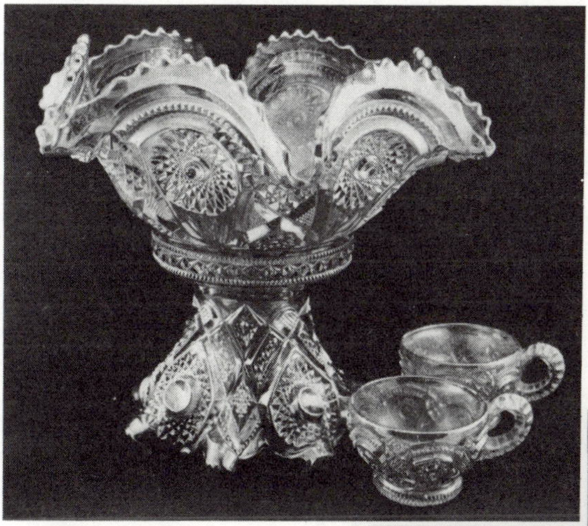

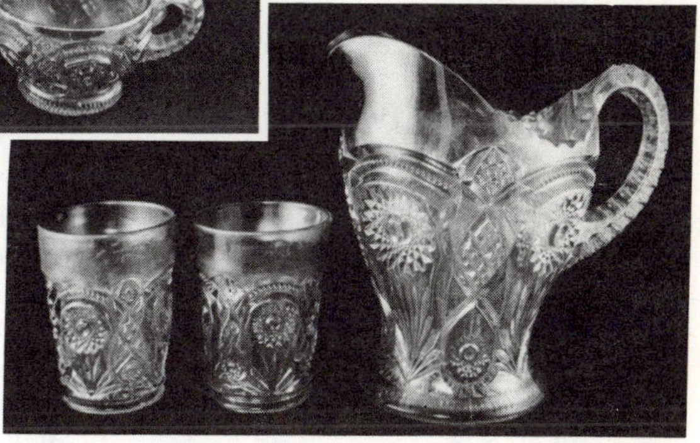

Pattern	Marigold	*Green, Blue, Amethyst, Purple*	Pastel	Red
FASHION				
Creamer	$ 50.00	$ 90.00	$140.00	
Sugar bowl	55.00	100.00	150.00	
Punch bowl	85.00	400.00		
Punch cup	15.00	45.00		
Pitcher	125.00	600.00	750.00	
Tumbler	25.00	125.00	125.00	
Bride's basket	125.00		175.00	

Pattern	Marigold	Green, Blue, Amethyst, Purple	Pastel	Red
FEATHER SCROLL				
Pitcher	$225.00	$350.00		
Tumbler	25.00	40.00		
FEATHER STITCH				
Bowl	$35.00	$45.00	$70.00	
FEATHERED SERPENT				
Bowl, 9"	$ 40.00	$ 50.00		
Bowl, 5"	20.00	25.00		
Fruit bowl	40.00	65.00		
Plate	125.00	200.00	$250.00	
FENTONIA				
Berry bowl, 9"	$ 40.00	$ 75.00		
Berry bowl, 5"	20.00	25.00		
Butter dish with cover	125.00	175.00		
Creamer	40.00	60.00		
Sugar bowl	45.00	65.00		
Spooner	40.00	60.00		
Pitcher	450.00	600.00		
Tumbler	60.00	100.00		
FETONIA FRUIT				
Bowl	$ 30.00	$ 40.00		
Tumbler	115.00	125.00		
FENTON'S ANIMALS (late)		$30.00		
FERN				
Bowl, 9"	$30.00	$50.00	$ 75.00	
Compote	25.00	55.00	100.00	
Hat	20.00	75.00	100.00	
FIELD THISTLE				
Butter dish with cover	$125.00	$150.00		
Creamer	40.00	55.00		
Sugar bowl	45.00	60.00		
Spooner	40.00	50.00		
Plate	55.00	100.00		
Pitcher	250.00	500.00		
Tumbler	65.00	125.00		

Pattern	Marigold	Green, Blue, Amethyst, Purple	Pastel	Red
FIELD FLOWER				
Milk pitcher	$125.00	$250.00		
Pitcher	150.00	350.00	$500.00	
Tumbler	25.00	75.00	125.00	

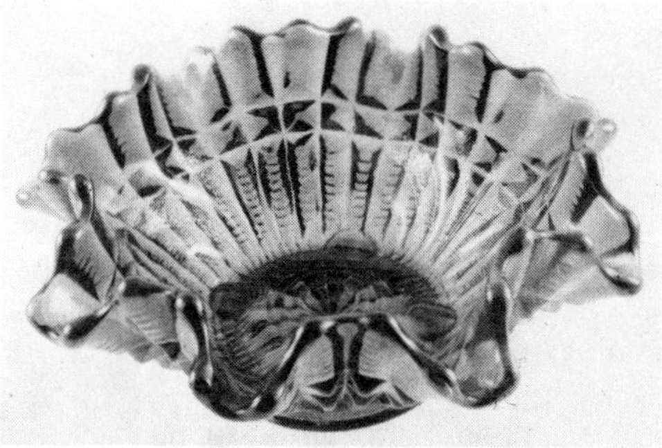

Pattern	Marigold	Green, Blue, Amethyst, Purple	Pastel	Red
FILE				
Bowl, 9"	$ 35.00	$ 45.00	$55.00	
Compote	35.00	45.00	55.00	
Pitcher	225.00	450.00		
FILE AND FAN				
Bowl	$40.00			
FINE CUT AND ROSES				
Rose bowl	$55.00	$70.00	$125.00 (ice white, ice blue)	
Candy dish	40.00	50.00	100.00	
FINE CUT FLOWERS				
Compote	$30.00			
FINE CUT HEART				
Berry bowl, 9"	$35.00	$50.00		
Bowl, 5"	20.00	25.00		
Fruit bowl	45.00	65.00		
FINE RIB				
Bowl, 9"	$30.00	$45.00		
Bowl, 5"	25.00	25.00		
Plate, 9"	25.00	35.00	$150.00	
Vase	20.00	25.00	75.00	$150.00
Bonbon	20.00	25.00		

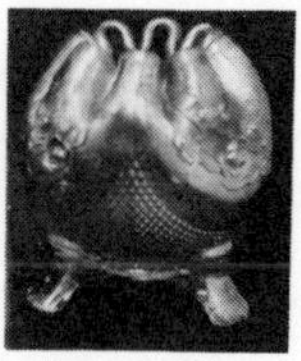

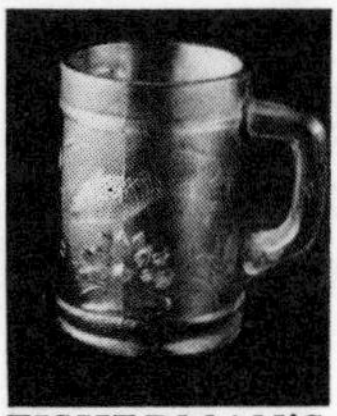

Pattern	Marigold	Green, Blue, Amethyst, Purple	Pastel	Red
FISHERMAN'S				
Mug	$150.00	$125.00		
FISHNET				
Epergne		800.00		
FISH SCALE AND BEADS				
Bonbon	$ 25.00	$40.00	$40.00	
Bride's basket	125.00			
Plate	35.00	65.00	65.00	
Lampshade			40.00	
FLEUR DE LIS				
Bowl	$65.00	$125.00		
Bowl, footed	75.00	150.00		
Vase	60.00			
FLORAL AND GRAPE				
Pitcher	$100.00	$250.00	$360.00	
Tumbler	45.00	60.00	75.00	
FLORAL AND OPTIC				
Bowl	$25.00	$40.00	$75.00	$225.00
Cake plate	40.00		75.00	
FLORAL OVAL				
Bowl, 9"	$30.00			
Sugar and creamer	65.00			
Plate, 7"	90.00			
FLOWERS AND FRAMES				
Bowl	$40.00	$75.00		
FLOWER FROGS (holders)	$15.00	$30.00		
	35.00	65.00		

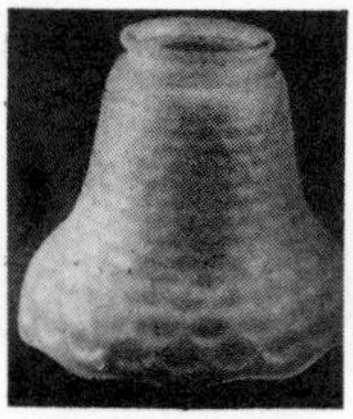

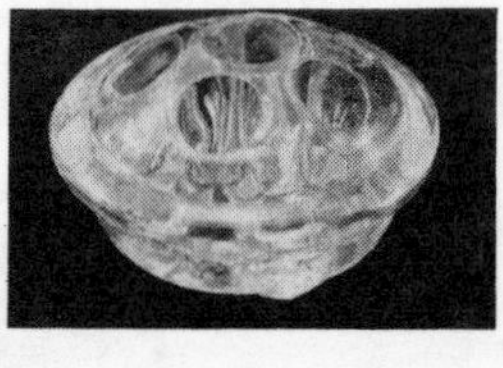

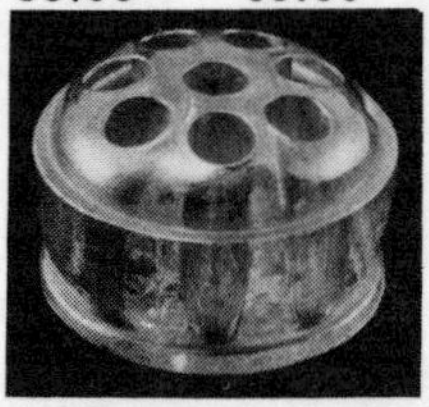

Pattern	Marigold	Green, Blue, Amethyst, Purple	Pastel	Red
FLOWERS AND SPADES				
Berry bowl, 9"	$50.00	$75.00		
Berry bowl, 5"	20.00	35.00		
FLUTE				
Bowl, 9"	$ 50.00	$100.00		
Bowl, 5"	20.00	35.00		
Butter dish with cover	150.00	200.00	$250.00 (ice white)	
Creamer	50.00	65.00	100.00	
Sugar bowl with lid	60.00	75.00	110.00	
Spooner	55.00	65.00	100.00	
Pitcher	200.00	250.00	350.00	
Tumbler	45.00	75.00	80.00	
Toothpick holder	60.00	100.00		
FOUR FLOWERS (also PODS AND POSIES)				
Bowl	$30.00	$ 55.00	$100.00 (peach opalescent)	
Plate	75.00	145.00		
Chop plate		400.00	500.00	
FOUR SEVENTY-FOUR				
Milk pitcher	$130.00	$450.00		
Punch bowl with stand	140.00	550.00		
Punch cup	20.00	45.00		
Pitcher	200.00	575.00		
Tumbler	55.00	100.00		
FROLICKING BEARS				
Pitcher		$6,000.00 (green)		
Tumbler		4,000.00		
FROSTED BLOCK				
Bowl, 9"	$25.00		$50.00	
Butter dish with cover	65.00			
Creamer	30.00			
Sugar bowl	35.00			
Plate	45.00		70.00	
Rose bowl	60.00		95.00	

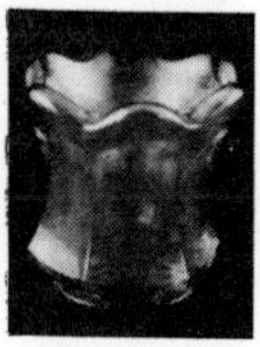

Pattern	Marigold	Green, Blue, Amethyst, Purple	Pastel	Red
FROSTED BUTTONS				
Bowl, footed			$200.00	
FROSTED RIBBON				
Pitcher	$125.00			
Tumbler	50.00			
FRUIT LUSTER				
Pitcher	$100.00			
Tumbler	25.00			

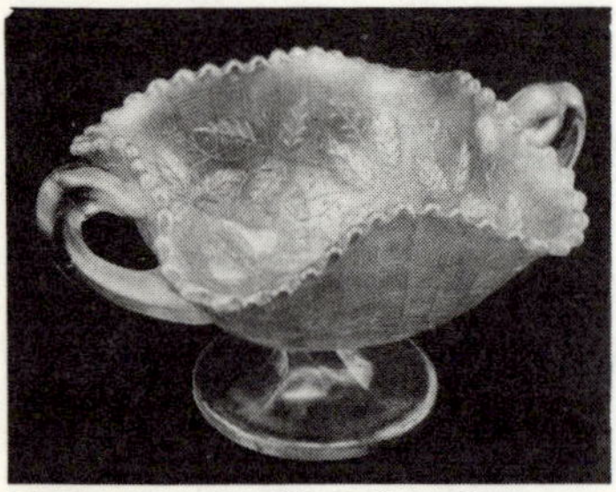

Pattern	Marigold	Green, Blue, Amethyst, Purple	Pastel	Red
FRUITS AND FLOWERS				
Bowl, 9"	$40.00	$ 50.00	$100.00	
Bowl, 5"	20.00	25.00	50.00	
Bonbon with stem	35.00	60.00	100.00	
Plate, 9"	70.00	115.00	170.00	
Fruit bowl	45.00	65.00	100.00	
GARDEN MUMS				
Bowl, 9"	$40.00	$ 55.00		
Bowl, 5"	20.00	35.00		
Plate	60.00	125.00		
GARDEN PATHS				
Bowl, 9"	$50.00	$100.00		
Chop plate		850.00	$1,000.00 (peach opalescent)	
Compote	35.00	55.00	100.00	
GARLAND				
Rose bowl	$75.00	$100.00		

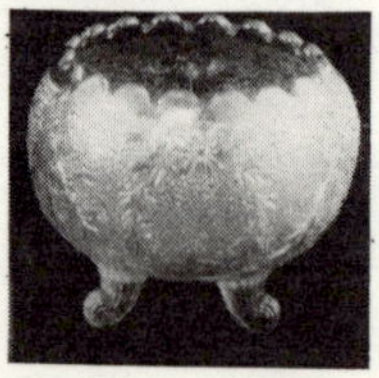

Pattern	Marigold	Green, Blue, Amethyst, Purple	Pastel	Red
GEORGIA BELLE				
Card tray	$45.00	$60.00		
Compote	45.00	60.00		
GOLD AND HOME				
Pitcher		$1,500.00 (blue)		
Tumbler		250.00		
GODDESS OF ATHENA				
Epergne	$3,500.00			
GOLDEN GRAPES				
Rose bowl,	$65.00			
Bowl, 8"	40.00			

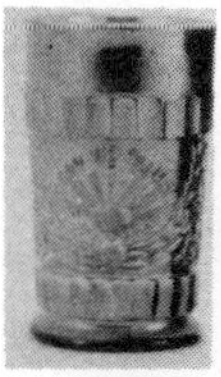

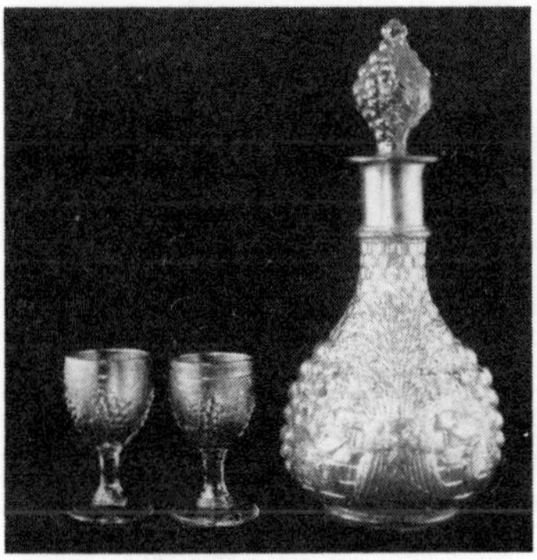

Pattern	Marigold	Green, Blue, Amethyst, Purple	Pastel	Red
GOLDEN HARVEST				
Wine decanter	$100.00	$250.00		
Wineglass	30.00	45.00		
GOLDEN WEDDING WHISKEY BOTTLE				
Quart	$15.00			
Pint	12.50			
Miniature	55.00			

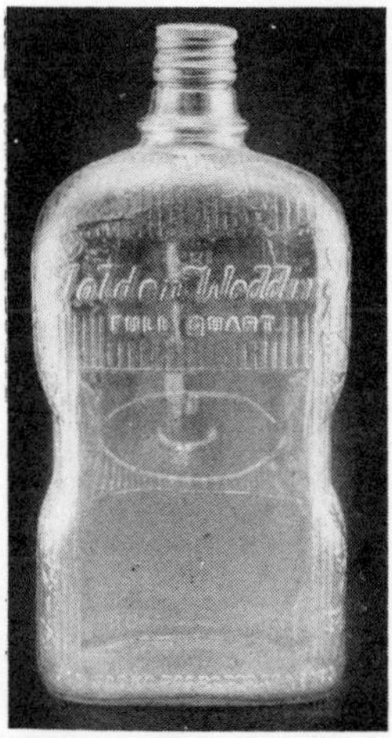

Pattern	Marigold	Green, Blue, Amethyst, Purple	Pastel	Red
GOOD LUCK				
Bowl, 9"	$100.00	$150.00	$300.00 (aqua opalescent)	
Plate, 9"	200.00	200.00	560.00 (aqua opalescent)	
GOOSEBERRY SPRAY				
Bowl, 9"	$55.00	$110.00	$125.00	
Bowl, 5"	25.00	50.00	75.00	
Compote		100.00	125.00	

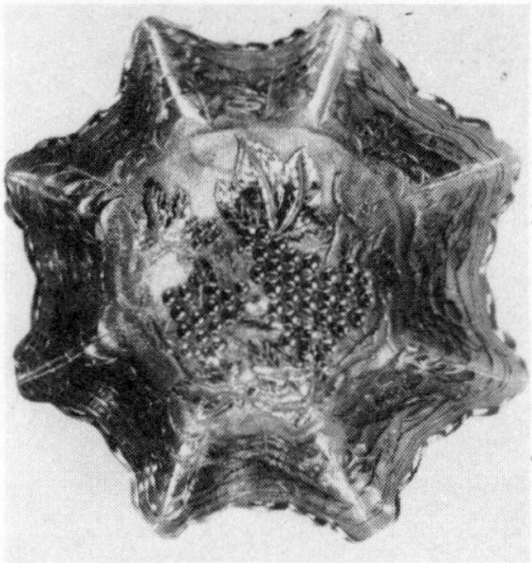

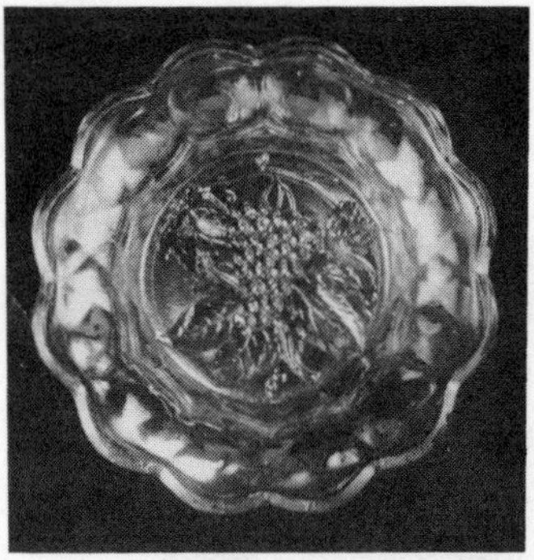

Pattern	Marigold	Green, Blue, Amethyst, Purple	Pastel	Red
GRAPE (FENTON)				
Bowl, 9"	$ 50.00	$100.00		
Bowl, 5"	25.00	40.00		
Chop plate, 12"	250.00	450.00	$500.00	
Plate, 7"	65.00	100.00		
GRAPE AND CABLE (FENTON)				
Orange bowl, footed	$125.00	$160.00		
Plate, footed, 9"				$500.00
GRAPE AND CABLE (NORTHWOOD)				
Banana Boat, footed, 12"	$160.00	$250.00	$ 350.00 1,500.00 (Vaseline base glass)	

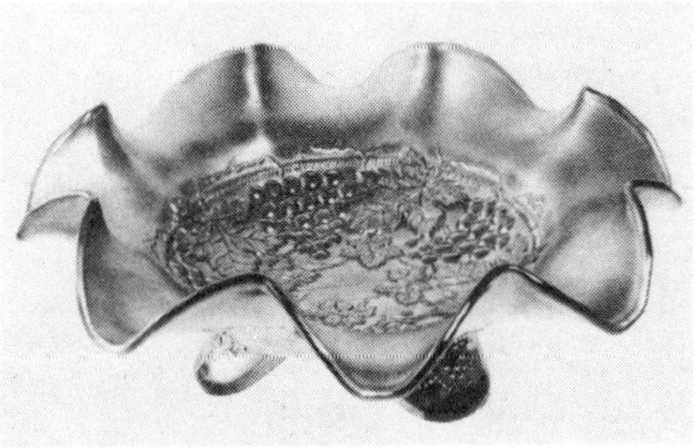

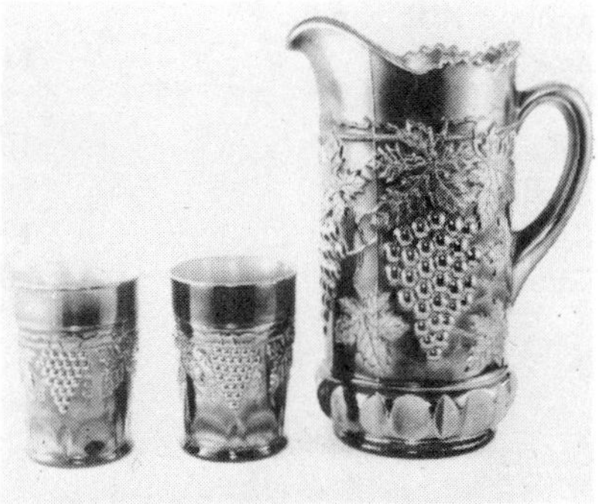

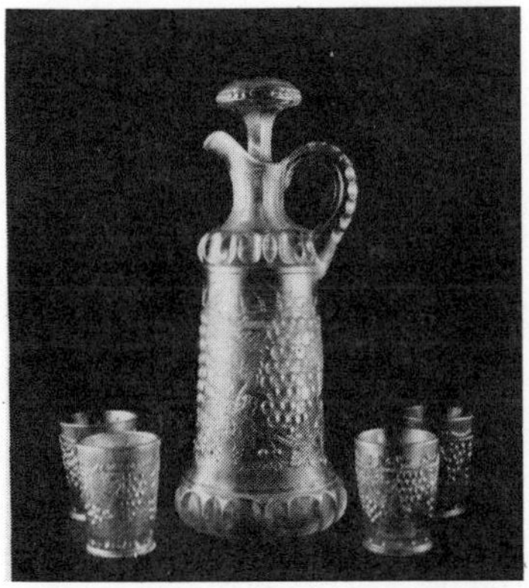

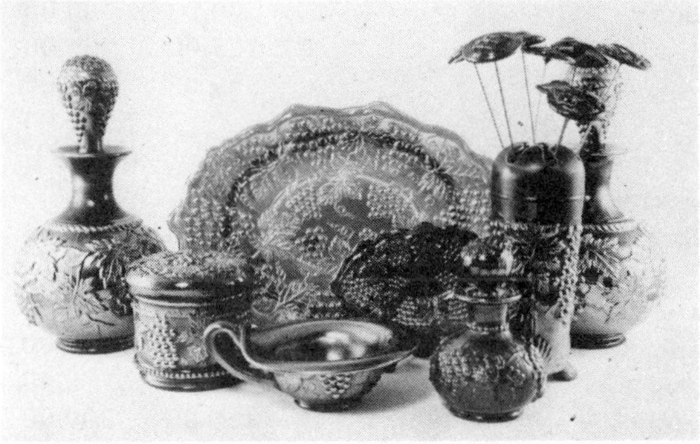

Pattern	Marigold	*Green, Blue, Amethyst, Purple*	Pastel	Red
Banquet punch bowl with stand	1,250.00	1,500.00	3,500.00 (ice blue)	
Banquet punch cup	35.00	45.00	75.00	
Bowl, 9"	50.00	65.00	150.00	
Bowl, 5"	20.00	25.00	45.00	
Bonbon with handles	35.00	45.00	65.00	
Bowl, 11"	110.00	160.00	250.00	
Bowl, 4½"	30.00	40.00	65.00	
Small creamer	100.00	100.00		
Small sugar bowl	100.00	110.00		
Candlesticks (pair)	175.00	225.00	450.00	
Candle lamp	600.00	600.00 (green) 800.00 (purple)		
Centerpiece bowl	300.00	350.00	500.00 (ice blue)	
Compote, covered	2,500.00	375.00		
Compote, open	500.00	500.00		
Compote, sweetmeat	725.00	250.00	500.00 (clambroth)	
Cookie jar with cover	155.00	350.00	700.00 (aqua opalescent) 1,500.00 (ice green)	
Butter dish with cover	175.00	200.00	300.00	
Creamer	75.00	100.00	175.00	
Sugar bowl	90.00	110.00	200.00	
Spooner	80.00	100.00	175.00	
Cup and saucer	225.00	225.00		
Cuspidor	550.00	550.00 7,500.00 (purple)		
Dresser set:				
Bottle (cologne)	125.00	175.00	375.00 (ice blue)	
Bottle (perfume)	600.00	550.00		
Hatpin holder	125.00	150.00	400.00	
Nappy	65.00	70.00	100.00	
Pin tray	150.00	200.00	300.00	
Powder jar with cover	65.00	100.00	275.00	
Tray (large)	175.00	200.00	350.00	

Pattern	Marigold	Green, Blue, Amethyst, Purple	Pastel	Red
Fernery	1,750.00	1,000.00	600.00	
			(white)	
Hat	20.00	40.00	60.00	
Ice cream dish, footed	30.00	45.00	75.00	
Orange bowl, footed	150.00	200.00	500.00	
Plate, 9"	60.00	100.00	125.00	
Plate, footed	100.00	150.00	250.00	
Punch bowl with stand	175.00	350.00	550.00	
			(white)	
Punch cup	20.00	25.00	55.00	
Tankard pitcher	600.00	600.00		
Tumbler	100.00	100.00		
Tobacco jar with cover	200.00	500.00	600.00	
			(ice blue)	
Water pitcher	300.00	350.00	500.00	
Tumbler	35.00	50.00	125.00	
Whiskey decanter	600.00	1,250.00		
Shot glasses	160.00	200.00		
GRAPE ARBOR				
Bowl, footed, 12"	$ 50.00	$100.00	$125.00	
Tall hat	35.00	55.00	100.00	
Rose bowl	65.00	110.00		
Pitcher	175.00	225.00	300.00	
Tumbler	45.00	75.00	100.00	
GRAPE DELIGHT				
Nut dish, footed	$60.00	$60.00	$100.00	
Rose bowl, footed	60.00	90.00	125.00	
			(white)	
GRAPE IMPERIAL				
Bowl, 10"	$ 35.00	$ 45.00		
Bowl, 5"	20.00	25.00		
Compote	30.00	50.00		
Cup and saucer	70.00	100.00		
Goblet	40.00	70.00		
Punch bowl	125.00	200.00		
Punch cup	25.00	35.00		
Water bottle	65.00	125.00		
		(purple)		
Pitcher	125.00	350.00		

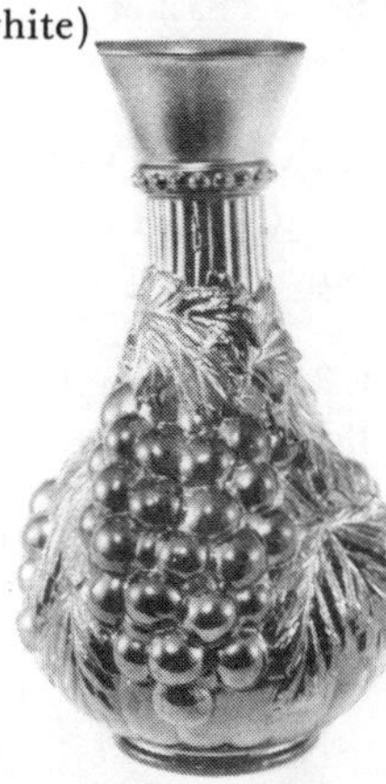

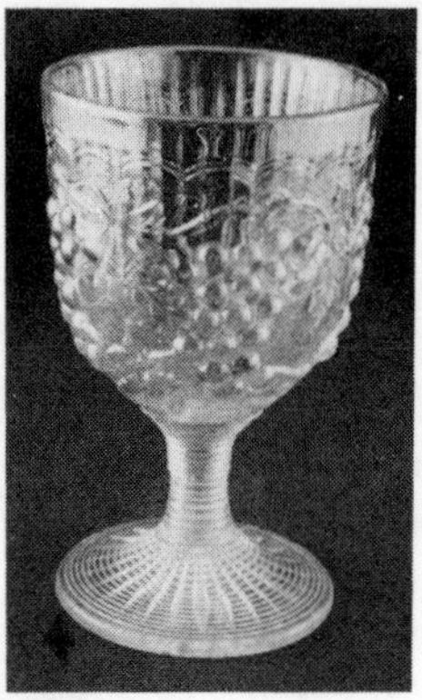

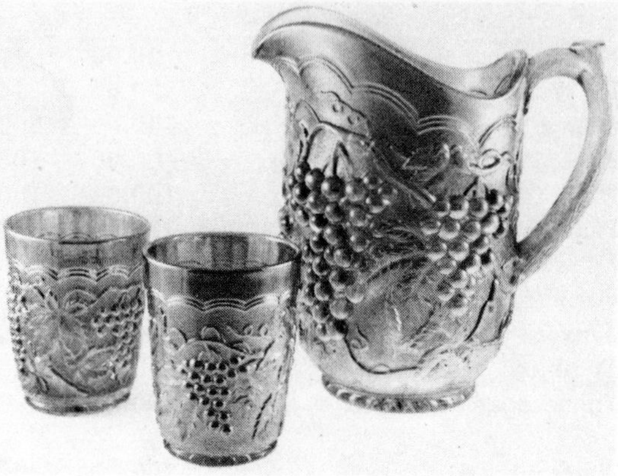

Pattern	Marigold	Green, Blue, Amethyst, Purple	Pastel	Red
Tumbler	$25.00	$ 60.00		
Wine decanter	70.00	200.00 (purple) 160.00 (green)		
Wineglass, stemmed	25.00	40.00 (purple) 35.00 (green)		
GRAPE LEAVES (NORTHWOOD)				
Bowl, 9"	$45.00	$ 55.00	$100.00	
Bride's basket	95.00	125.00		
Plate	75.00	100.00	135.00	
GRAPE LEAVES AND ACORNS				
Bowl	$75.00	$100.00		
GRAPE WREATH				
Bowl	$35.00	$50.00		
GRAPE AND CHERRY				
Bowl	$35.00			

Pattern	Marigold	*Green, Blue, Amethyst, Purple*	Pastel	Red
GRAPE AND GOTHIC ARCHES				
Bowl, 9"	$ 30.00	$ 45.00		
Bowl, 5"	15.00	20.00		
Butter dish with cover	100.00	170.00		
Creamer	40.00	50.00		
Sugar bowl	45.00	55.00		
Spooner	40.00	50.00		
Pitcher	150.00	200.00		
Tumbler	40.00	60.00		

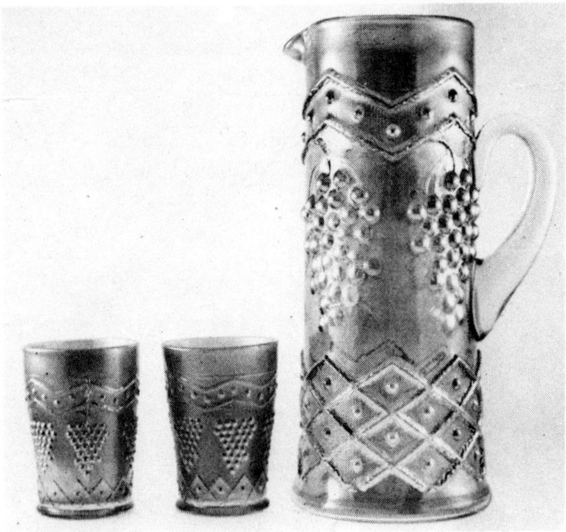

GRAPE AND LATTICE				
Pitcher	$150.00	$200.00		
Tumbler	35.00	55.00		
GRAPE AND LEAVES				
Gone-with-the-winde lamp	$2,000.00			

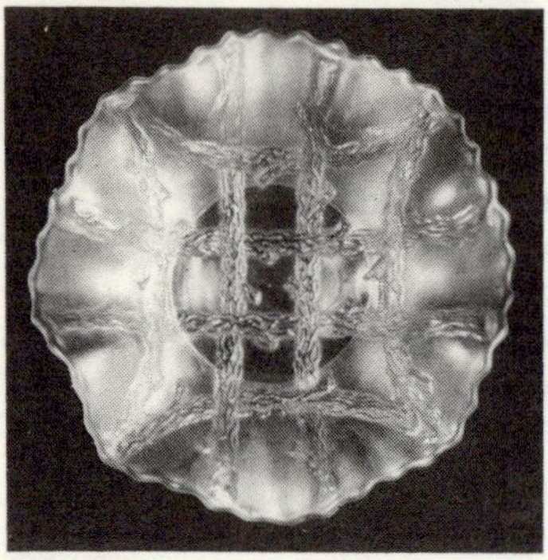

GRAPEVINE LATTICE	Marigold	Green, Blue, Amethyst, Purple	Pastel	Red
Bowl, 8"	$ 40.00	$ 50.00		
Plate, 7"	50.00	75.00	$100.00	
Pitcher	200.00	260.00	375.00	
Tumbler	45.00	55.00	100.00	

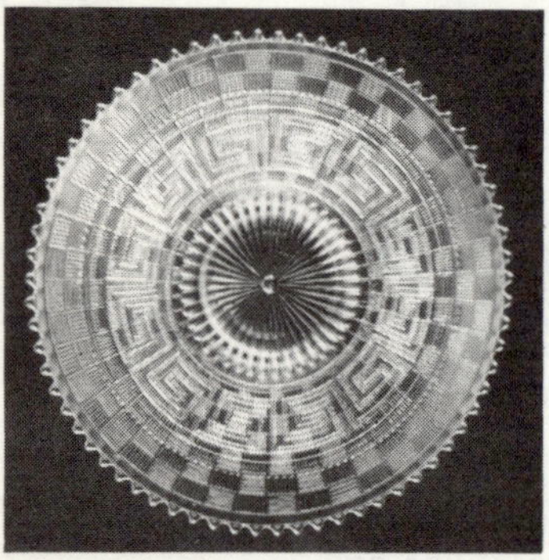

GREEK KEY	Marigold	Green, Blue, Amethyst, Purple	Pastel	Red
Bowl, flat, 9"	$ 35.00	$ 55.00		
Bowl, footed, 9"	50.00	75.00		
Pitcher	350.00	650.00		
Plate, 9"	150.00	275.00		
Tumbler	100.00	100.00		

Pattern	Marigold	Green, Blue, Amethyst, Purple	Pastel	Red

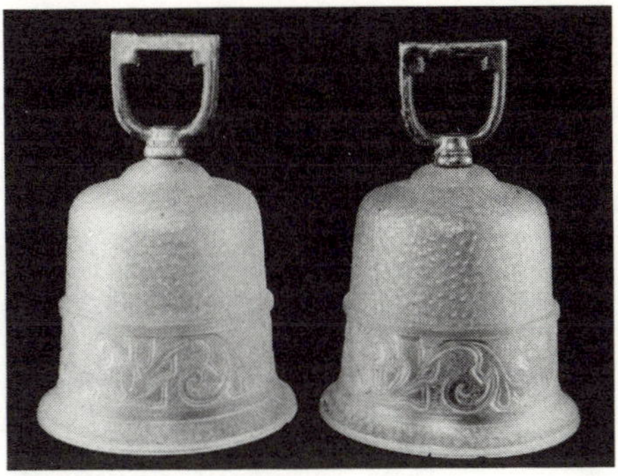

HAMMERED BELL CHANDELIER				
Complete, five shades			$1,500.00	
Shades, each			200.00	
HARVEST FLOWER				
Tumbler	$50.00	$100.00		
HARVEST POPPY				
Compote	$30.00	$50.00		
HATPINS (all patterns)	$25.00	$35.00		
HATTIE				
Bowl	$ 30.00	$ 40.00	$100.00	
Chop plate	200.00	300.00	400.00	
Rose bowl	100.00			
HEART AND HORSESHOE				
Bowl	$ 70.00	$100.00		
Plate	125.00	200.00		
HEART AND FEATHER				
Compote	$ 55.00			
Pitcher	300.00			
Tumbler	75.00			

Pattern	Marigold	Green, Blue, Amethyst, Purple	Pastel	Red
HEARTS AND FLOWERS				
Bowl, 9"	$ 40.00	$ 50.00	$100.00 (ice blue)	
Compote	40.00	50.00	200.00 (aqua opalescent)	
Plate, 9"	150.00	250.00	300.00 (ice blue)	
HEART AND STAR				
Handled basket	$175.00			
HEART AND VINE				
Bowl, 9"	$35.00	$ 45.00	$ 75.00	
Plate, 9"	65.00	125.00	200.00	
HEART BAND				
Mug	$100.00			
Salt dip	75.00			
HEARTS AND TREES				
Bowl, 9"	$ 40.00	$ 55.00	$100.00	
Compote	40.00	50.00	125.00	
Plate, 9"	150.00	175.00	250.00	
Pitcher	175.00	300.00		
Tumbler	75.00	100.00		
HEAVY DIAMOND				
Bowl, 9"	$25.00			
Creamer	20.00			
Sugar bowl	25.00			

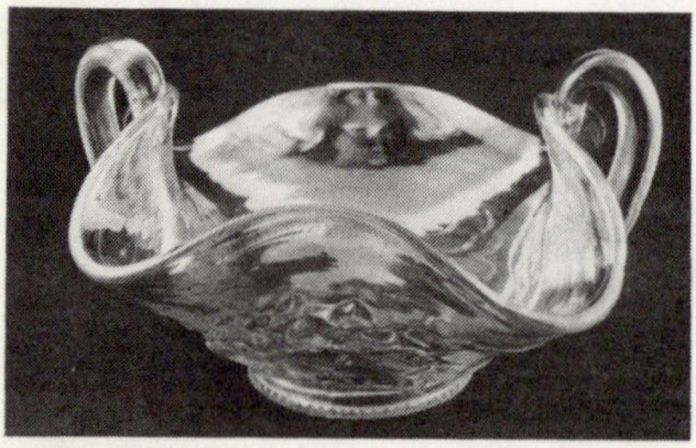

HEAVY HOBNAIL				
Candy dish			$300.00 (white)	

Pattern	Marigold	Green, Blue, Amethyst, Purple	Pastel	Red
HEAVY PRISMS				
Celery holder	$65.00			
HEAVY SHELL				
Bowl			$140.00	
HERON				
Mug	$125.00	$175.00		
HEXAGON CANDLESTICKS				$425.00
HICKMAN CASTOR SET (miniature)	$500.00			

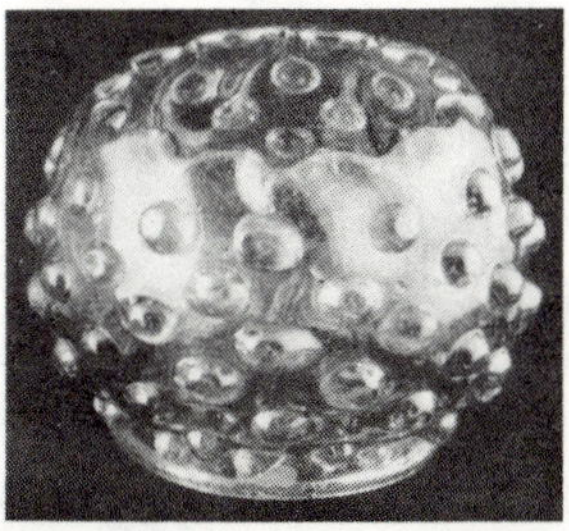

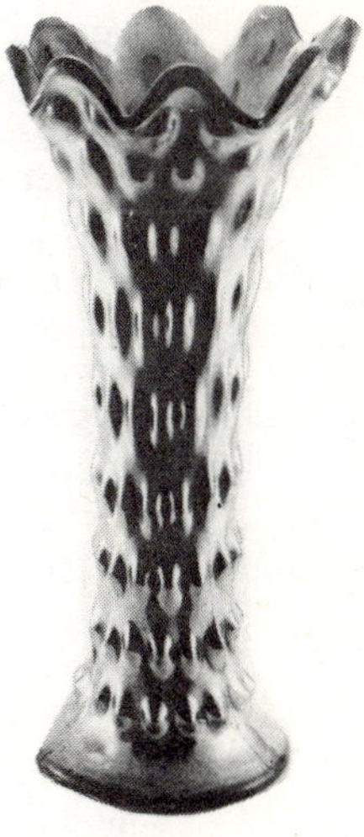

Pattern	Marigold	Green, Blue, Amethyst, Purple	Pastel	Red
HOBNAIL (MILLERSBURG)				
Rose bowl	$150.00	$175.00		
Spittoon	250.00	350.00		
HOBNAIL (NORTHWOOD)				
Butter dish with cover	$150.00	$200.00		
Creamer	60.00	100.00		
Sugar bowl	75.00	110.00		
Spooner	60.00	100.00		
Pitcher	275.00	400.00		
Tumbler	65.00	100.00		
Vase, various sizes	30.00	35.00		
	75.00	100.00		
HOBNAIL SODA GOLD				
Spittoon	$45.00		$275.00 (marigold on pale green)	

Pattern	Marigold	Green, Blue Amethyst, Purple	Pastel	Red

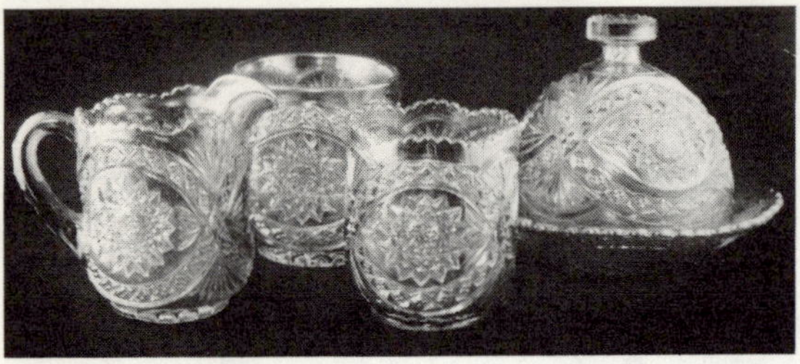

Pattern	Marigold	Green, Blue Amethyst, Purple	Pastel	Red
HOBSTAR (IMPERIAL)				
Butter dish	$75.00	$200.00		
Creamer	30.00	50.00		
Sugar bowl	35.00	55.00		
Spooner	30.00	50.00		
HOBSTAR AND ARCHES				
Bowl, 9"	$ 40.00	$ 75.00		
Centerpiece fruit bowl	125.00	150.00		
HOBSTAR BAND				
Pitcher	$135.00	$200.00		
Tumbler	45.00	75.00		
HOBSTAR AND FEATHER				
Banquet punch bowl	$2,250.00	$2,500.00		
Punch cup	60.00	115.00		
Giant rose bowl		1,250.00		
Table set (4 pieces)		1,500.00		
HOBSTAR AND FRUIT				
Bowl	$45.00			
HOBSTAR FLOWER				
Compote	$40.00			
HOLIDAY				
Tray	$250.00			
HOLLY WHIRL (or SPRIG)				
Nappy	$35.00	$65.00	$55.00	
Bonbon	40.00	55.00	45.00	
Bowl, 9"	45.00	65.00		
Sauce boat	45.00	65.00		
Hat	40.00	55.00	50.00	

Pattern	Marigold	Green, Blue, Amethyst, Purple	Pastel	Red

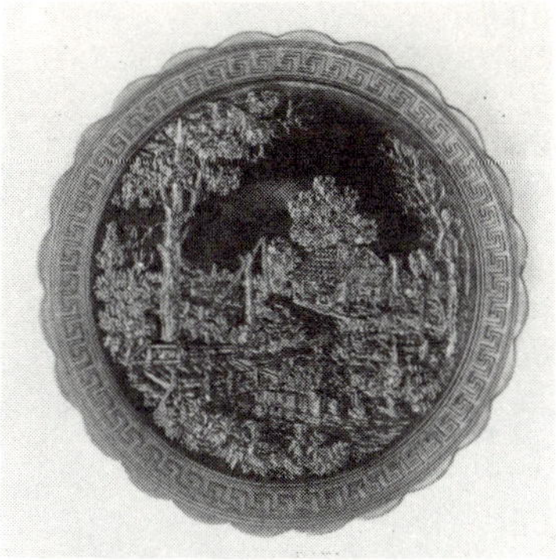

HOMESTEAD (NU-ART)				
Plate, 10"	$600.00	$650.00	$800.00	

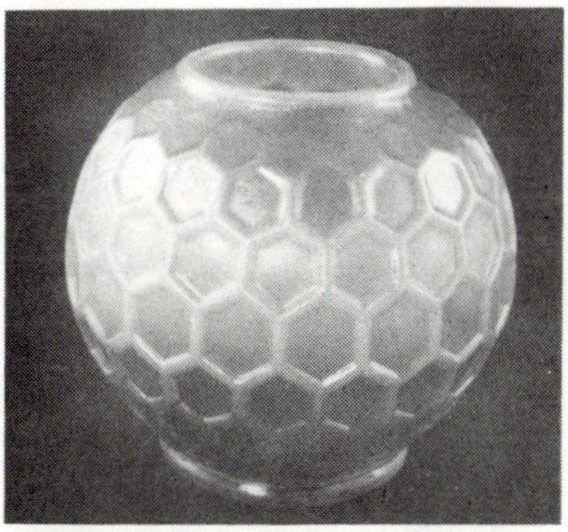

HONEYCOMB				
Rose bowl			$150.00 (peach opalescent)	
HONEYCOMB AND CLOVER				
Bonbon	$25.00	$30.00		
HORSE MEDALLION				
Candy dish	$ 75.00	$100.00		
Plate, 8"	100.00	125.00	$150.00	
Rose bowl	125.00	150.00		
HORSESHOE CURVE				
Compote	$50.00	$65.00		
HORSESHORE SHOT GLASS	$150.00			

Pattern	Marigold	Green, Blue, Amethyst, Purple	Pastel	Red
HYACINTH LAMP	$2,500.00			
ILLINOIS DAISY				
Bowl, 9"	$ 50.00			
Tobacco jar with cover	100.00			
ILLUSION				
Bonbon	$45.00	$100.00		
Bowl, 8"	35.00	75.00		
INTAGLIO DAISY				
Bowl, 9"	$50.00			
Bowl, 5"	25.00			
INVERTED COIN DOT				
Pitcher	$175.00	$400.00		
Tumbler	40.00	80.00		
INVERTED FEATHER				
Cracker jar with lid		$200.00		
Butter dish with cover	$125.00	225.00		
Creamer	45.00	95.00		
Sugar bowl	50.00	100.00		
Spooner	45.00	90.00		
Pitcher	225.00	700.00		
Tumbler	60.00	85.00		
INVERTED STRAWBERRY				
Bowl, 9"	$ 60.00	$100.00		
Bowl, 5"	35.00	50.00		
Candlesticks (pair)	225.00	300.00		
Compote	200.00	250.00		
Butter dish with cover	175.00	250.00		
Creamer	100.00	125.00		
Sugar bowl	110.00	150.00		
Spooner	100.00	125.00		
Cuspidor	500.00	500.00		
Pitcher	300.00	750.00		
Tumbler	100.00	135.00		
Powder jar	100.00	125.00		

Pattern	Marigold	Green, Blue, Amethyst, Purple	Pastel	Red
INVERTED THISTLE				
Small spittoon	$500.00	$ 500.00		
Box with cover	100.00	115.00		
Pitcher	300.00	1,000.00		
Tumbler	100.00	125.00		
INVERTED THUMBPRINT				
Vase	$45.00			
IRIS, HEAVY				
Pitcher	$300.00	$900.00	$1,250.00	
Tumbler	75.00	100.00	125.00	
IRIS AND HERRINGBONE				
Plate, 9"	$ 8.50			
Plate, 8"	7.00			
Plate, 5½"	6.00			
Bowl, 6"	7.00			
Bowl, 5"	7.00			
Bowl, 4½"	6.00			
Cup and saucer	15.00			
Tumbler, footed, 7"	12.50			
Tumbler, footed, 6"	12.50			
Tumbler, 4"	9.00			
Goblet, 7"	15.00			
Goblet, 5¾"	15.00			
Goblet, 4½"	15.00			
Sherbet, 4"	8.00			
Sherbet, 3½"	8.00			
Coaster, 3½"	5.00			
Plate, 12"	17.50			
Bowl, fluted edge	15.00			
Bowl, 11"	15.00			
Pitcher	30.00			
Butter dish with cover	30.00			
Candy jar with cover	45.00			
Creamer	10.00			
Sugar bowl with cover	15.00			
Candlesticks (pair)	35.00			
Vase	35.00			

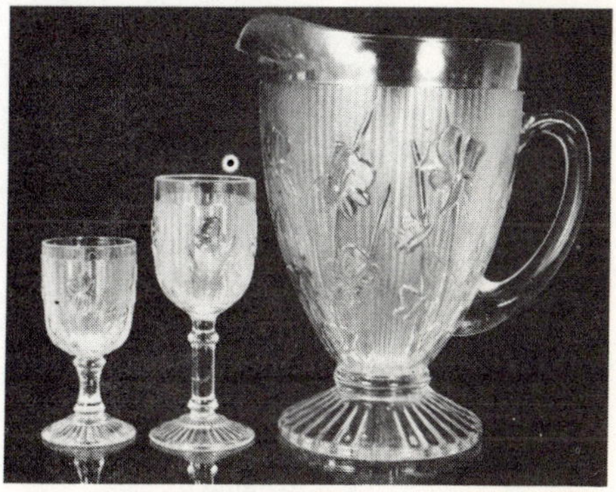

Pattern	Marigold	Green, Blue, Amethyst, Purple	Pastel	Red

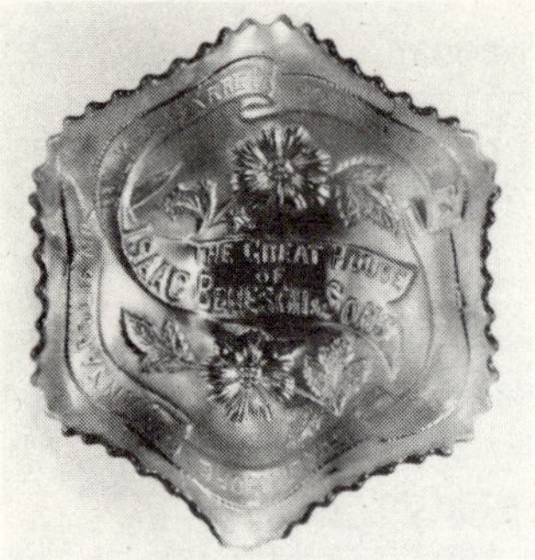

Pattern	Marigold	Green, Blue, Amethyst, Purple	Pastel	Red
ISAAC BENESCH				
Bowl		$225.00		
JACK-IN-THE-PULPIT				
Vase	$40.00	$45.00	$70.00 (peach opalescent)	
JEWELED HEART				
Bowl, 10"	$ 30.00	$ 50.00	$100.00	
Bowl, 5"	15.00	20.00	35.00	
Plate, 7"	30.00	40.00		
Pitcher	240.00	550.00	625.00	
Tumbler	75.00	100.00	135.00	
JOCKEY CLUB		$130.00		

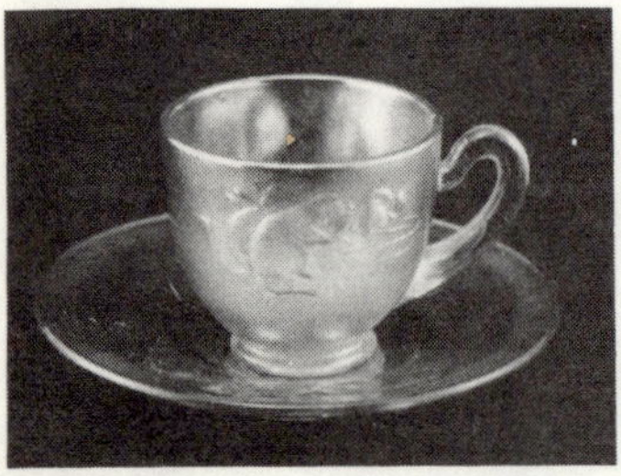

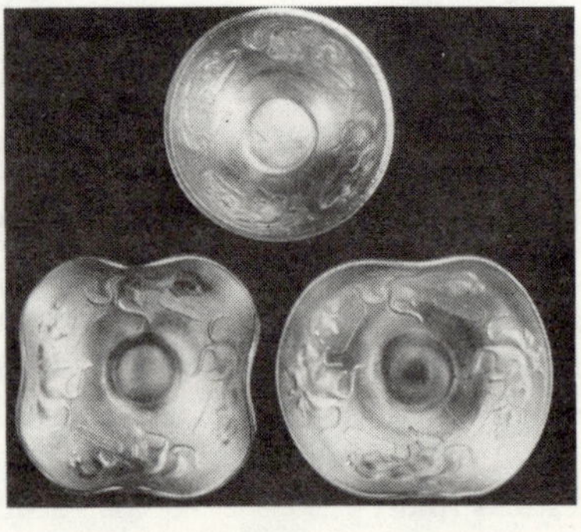

Pattern	Marigold	Green, Blue, Amethyst, Purple	Pastel	Red
KITTENS (miniatures)				
Bowl, oval	$100.00	$110.00	$125.00	
Bowl, round, square	65.00	80.00	100.00	
Cup and saucer	200.00	225.00	225.00	

Pattern	Marigold	Green, Blue, Amethyst, Purple	Pastel	Red
Cuspidor (or rose bowl)	$2,500.00			
Spooner	100.00	$150.00	$150.00	
Toothpick holder	100.00	125.00	125.00	
KNIGHTS TEMPLAR				
Mug	$275.00	$350.00	$400.00	
KOKOMO				
Rose bowl	$55.00	$75.00		

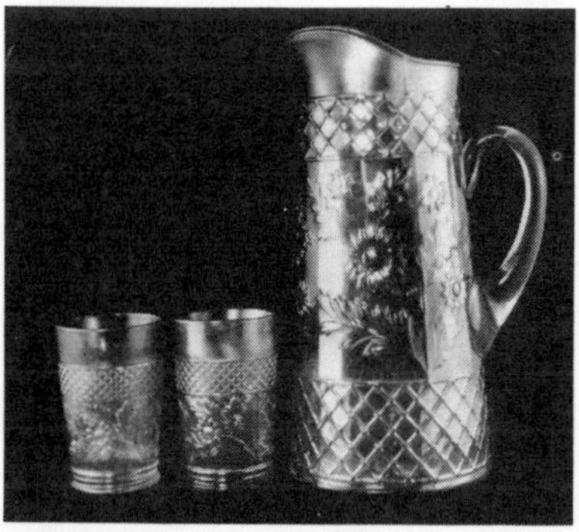

Pattern	Marigold	Green, Blue, Amethyst, Purple	Pastel	Red
LATTICE AND DAISY				
Bowl, 9"	$ 40.00			
Bowl, 5"	15.00			
Pitcher	125.00	$300.00		
Tumbler	45.00	50.00		
LEAF AND BANDS				
Candy dish, footed	$30.00	$ 60.00		
Rose bowl, footed	45.00	100.00	$150.00 (aqua opalescent)	
Plate, 7"	50.00	75.00	125.00	
LEAF AND BEADS				
Bowl	$30.00	$40.00		
Rose bowl	40.00	50.00		
LEAF CHAIN				
Bonbon	$25.00	$35.00		
Bowl, 9"	35.00	40.00	$ 90.00	
Plate, 9"	70.00	90.00	110.00	

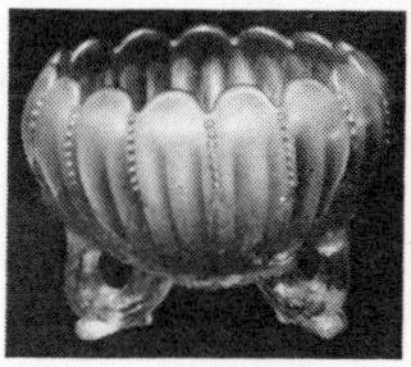

Pattern	Marigold	Green, Blue, Amethyst, Purple	Pastel	Red
LEAF COLUMN				
Light shade			$100.00	
Vase	$30.00	$35.00		
LEAF RAYS				
Nappy	$25.00	$30.00	65.00	
LEAF SWIRL				
Bowl, 9"	$30.00	$37.50		
Compote	30.00	37.50	$85.00	

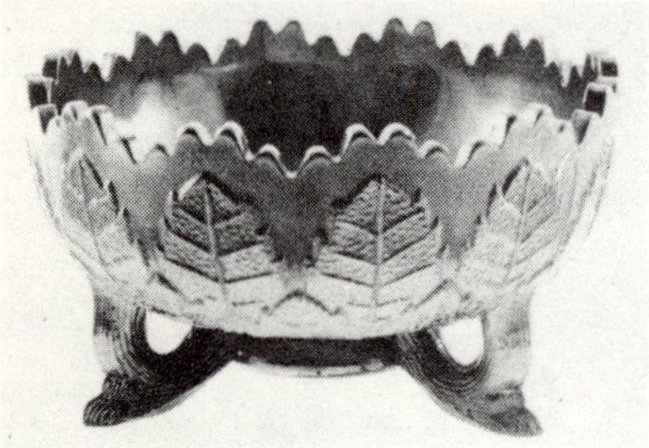

Pattern	Marigold	Green, Blue, Amethyst, Purple	Pastel	Red
LEAF TIERS				
Bowl, 9"	$ 40.00			
Bowl, 5"	20.00			
Butter dish with cover	125.00			
Creamer	40.00			
Sugar bowl	45.00			
Spooner	40.00			
Pitcher	300.00	$600.00		
Tumbler	65.00	100.00		
LILY OF THE VALLEY				
Pitcher	$2,000.00	$2,250.00	$2,750.00	
Tumbler	225.00	250.00	300.00	
LINED LATTICE				
Vase	$30.00	$40.00	$75.00	

Pattern	Marigold	*Green, Blue, Amethyst, Purple*	Pastel	Red

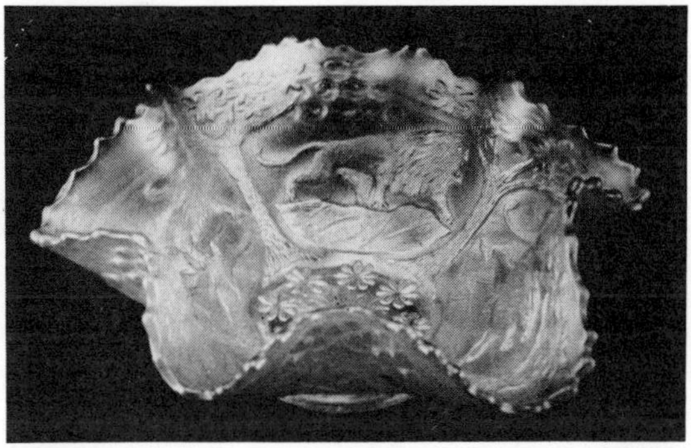

LION				
Bowl, 8"	$100.00	$150.00		
Plate, 7"	275.00	350.00		
LITTLE BEADS				
Bowl	$45.00	$45.00		
Small compote	50.00			
LITTLE FERNERY				
Nut dish	$50.00	$50.00		$250.00

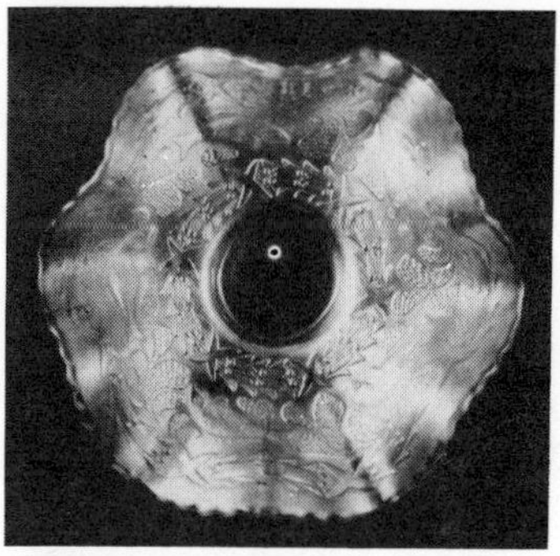

LITTLE FISHES				
Bowl, footed, 9"	$150.00	$250.00		
Bowl, footed, 5"	75.00	100.00		
Plate, 7"		400.00	$475.00	

Pattern	Marigold	Green, Blue, Amethyst, Purple	Pastel	Red
LITTLE FLOWERS				
Bowl, 9"	$ 35.00	$ 60.00		
Bowl, 5"	20.00	30.00		
Rose bowl	60.00	100.00		
Plate, large	250.00	350.00		
LITTLE ORANGE TREE				
Creamer	$125.00	$125.00		
Sugar bowl	150.00	150.00		
LITTLE STARS				
Bowl, 8"	$40.00	$75.00		

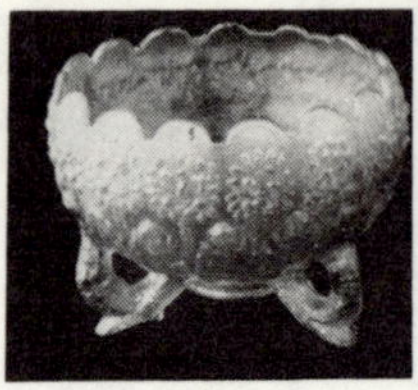

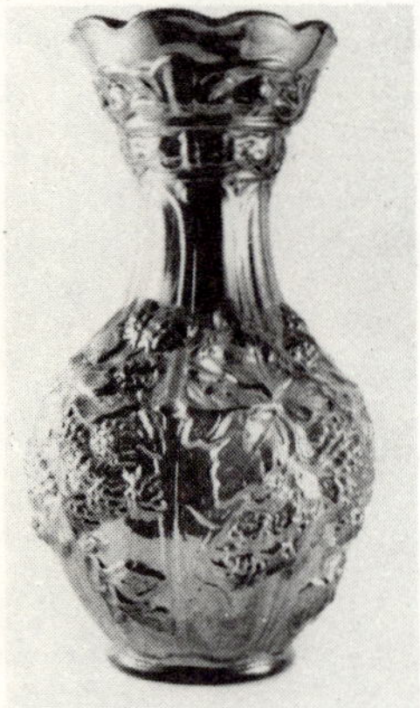

Pattern	Marigold	Green, Blue, Amethyst, Purple	Pastel	Red
LOGANBERRY				
Vase	$200.00	$300.00	$475.00	
LONG HOBSTAR				
Bowl, 8"	$35.00			
Compote, large	45.00			
LONG LEAF				
Bowl	$25.00			
LONG THUMBPRINT				
Bowl, 8"	$30.00	$40.00		
Compote	30.00	40.00		
Creamer	30.00	30.00		
Sugar bowl	35.00	35.00		

Pattern	Marigold	Green, Blue, Amethyst, Purple	Pastel	Red
LOTUS AND GRAPE				
Bonbon	$ 25.00	$ 35.00		
Bowl, 9"	35.00	50.00		
Plate, 8"	100.00	175.00		
LOTUS AND POINSETTIA				
Bowl	$90.00	$110.00		

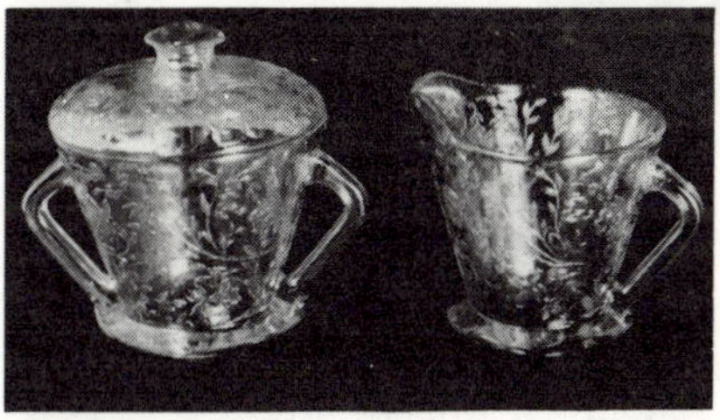

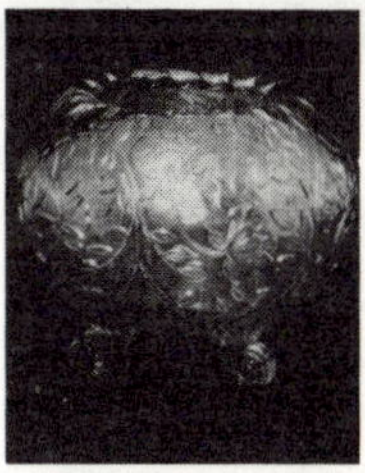

LOUISA				
Rose bowl	$45.00	$65.00		
Bowl, 9"	15.00	35.00		
Nut bowl, footed	20.00	25.00		
Sauce bowl, footed	15.00	20.00		
Sugar bowl and creamer	25.00			
Pitcher	50.00			
Tumbler	15.00			
LUSTER FLUTE				
Bowl, 8"	$15.00	$ 20.00		
Candy dish		20.00		
Creamer	25.00	40.00		
Sugar bowl	30.00	50.00		
Hat	15.00	20.00		
Punch bowl with stand		425.00		
Punch cup		30.00		
LUSTER ROSE				
Bowl, 7"-9"	$25.00	$ 35.00		
Bowl, footed, 10"	30.00	40.00		
Butter dish with cover	65.00	125.00		
Creamer	25.00	45.00		
Sugar bowl	30.00	50.00		
Spooner	25.00	45.00		
Fernery, footed	40.00	75.00		

Pattern	Marigold	*Green, Blue, Amethyst, Purple*	Pastel	Red

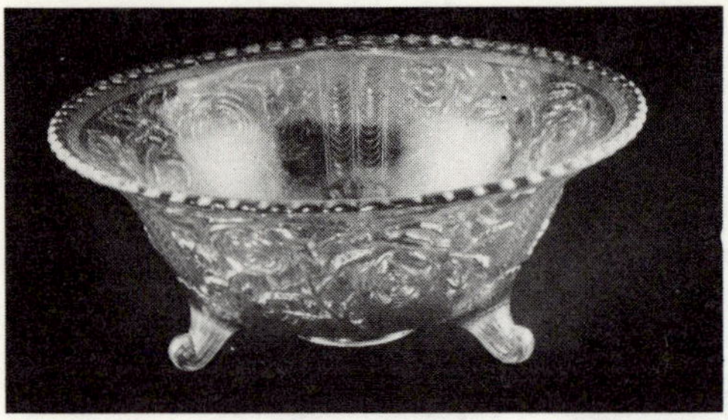

Pitcher	$100.00	$225.00		
Tumbler	30.00	50.00		
Plate, 9"	50.00	65.00		
MALAGA				
Bowl, 9"	$ 75.00	$100.00		
Plate	100.00	125.00		
MANY FRUITS				
Punch bowl with stand	$250.00	$375.00		
Punch cup	25.00	35.00		
MANY STARS				
Bowl, 9"	$100.00	$150.00		
Plate, 9"	125.00	250.00		
MAPLE LEAF				
Bowl, footed	$ 75.00	$125.00		
Bowl, small footed	20.00	30.00		
Basket with handles	175.00			
Bowl, 9"	65.00	100.00		
Bowl, 5"	25.00	40.00		
Butter dish with cover	125.00	175.00		
Creamer	30.00	45.00		
Sugar bowl	35.00	50.00		
Spooner	30.00	40.00		
Pitcher	175.00	300.00		
Tumbler	30.00	55.00		
MARILYN				
Pitcher	$750.00	$1,250.00		
Tumbler	100.00	200.00		

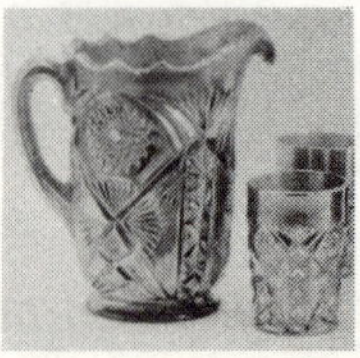

Pattern	Marigold	Green, Blue, Amethyst, Purple	Pastel	Red

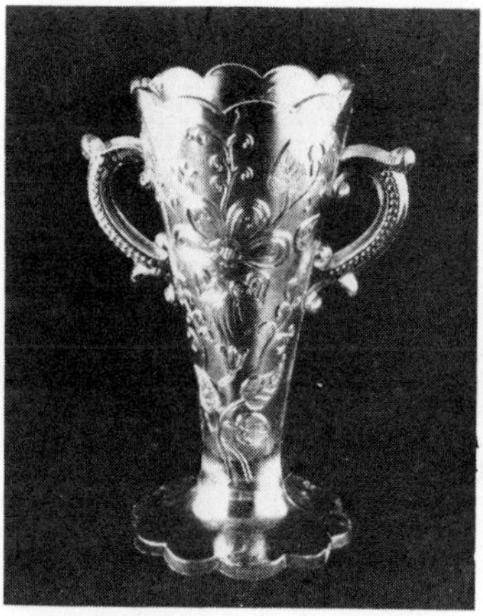

MARY ANN				
Vase	$ 50.00	$100.00		
Vase, 3 handles	100.00	200.00		
MAYAN				
Bowl, 9"	$30.00	$ 50.00		
Plate, 9"		250.00		
MAY BASKET	$75.00			
MAYFLOWER				
Bowl	$ 25.00	$ 40.00	$50.00	
Compote	25.00	40.00	40.00	
Pitcher	250.00	350.00		
Tumbler	35.00	75.00		
Hat shape	20.00	30.00	25.00	
MELON RIB				
Candy jar with cover	$ 25.00			
Powder jar with cover	25.00			
Cordial set				
Decanter	75.00			
Glass	15.00			
Spittoon	200.00			

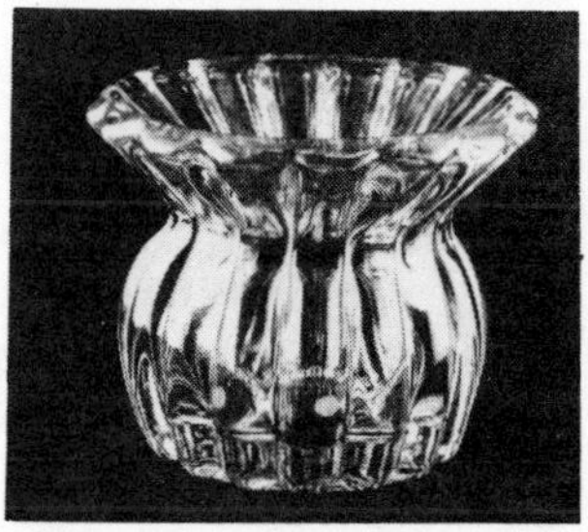

Pattern	Marigold	Green, Blue, Amethyst, Purple	Pastel	Red
MEMPHIS				
Fruit bowl, 12"	$ 50.00	$ 75.00	$200.00	
Punch bowl with stand	200.00	300.00	550.00 (ice blue)	
Punch cup	35.00	45.00	125.00	
MIKADO				
Bowl, 10"	$ 45.00	$ 75.00		
Compote	150.00	250.00		
MILADY				
Pitcher	$200.00	$700.00	$625.00	
Tumbler	65.00	85.00	75.00	

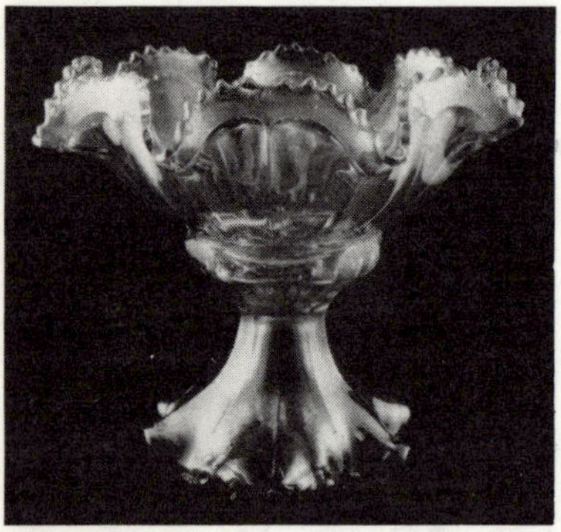

Pattern	Marigold	Green, Blue, Amethyst, Purple	Pastel	Red
MILLERSBURG FLUTE				
Punch bowl	$300.00			
Cup	55.00			
Bowl, 4"		$65.00		
MILLERSBURG GAY NINETIES				
Pitcher	$4,000.00	$4,000.00		
Tumbler	550.00	525.00		
MILLERSBURG WILD ROSE AND HONEYCOMB LAMP				
Lamp without medallions	$ 600.00	$ 750.00		
Lamp with medallions in base	1,500.00	1,250.00		

Pattern	Marigold	Green, Blue, Amethyst, Purple	Pastel	Red
MIRRORED LOTUS				
Bonbon	$25.00	$30.00	$ 60.00	
Bowl, 8"	25.00	42.50		
Plate, 7"	50.00	70.00	100.00	
MORNING GLORY				
Pitcher	$5,000.00	$6,000.00		
Tumbler	500.00	725.00		
MORNING GLORY AND DRAPE				
Bowl, 9"			$75.00 (peach opalescent)	
MULTI-FRUITS AND FLOWERS				
Punch bowl	$ 300.00	$ 400.00		
Punch cup	30.00	35.00		
Pitcher	7,000.00	6,500.00 (amethyst)		
Tumbler	200.00	200.00		

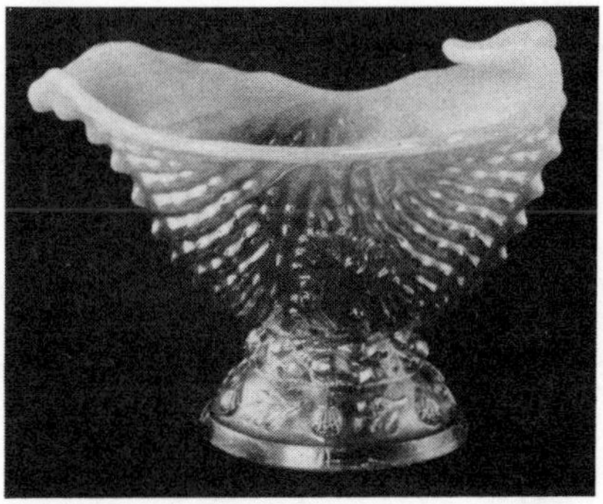

NAUTILUS SAUCEBOAT				
One mold, two shapes	$200.00	$150.00 (peach opalescent)		
Signed	250.00	175.00		

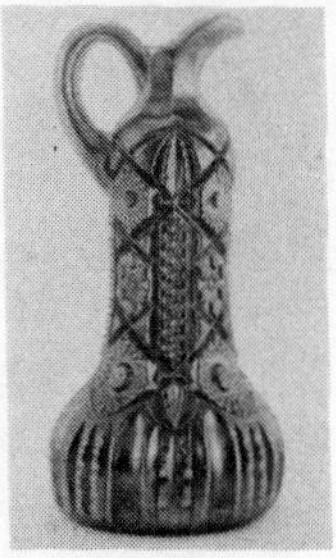

Pattern	Marigold	Green, Blue, Amethyst, Purple	Pastel	Red
NEAR-CUT DECANTER		$800.00		
NESTING SWAN				
Bowl	$150.00	$250.00		
NIPPON				
Bowl	$45.00	$55.00	$100.00 (ice blue)	
NORTHERN STAR				
Bonbon	$20.00			
Bowl	15.00			
OCTAGON				
Butter dish with cover	$100.00	$130.00		
Creamer	40.00	55.00		
Sugar bowl	45.00	65.00		
Spooner	40.00	55.00		
Goblet	30.00			
Toothpick holder	100.00	120.00		
Wine decanter	70.00	250.00		
Wineglass, stemmed	30.00	40.00		
OCTET				
Bowl, footed	$45.00	$60.00	$75.00	
OHIO STAR				
Vase	$50.00	$60.00	$65.00	
OKLAHOMA				
Tumble-up, water set	$125.00			
Pitcher	125.00			
Tumbler	35.00			

Pattern	Marigold	Green, Blue, Amethyst, Purple	Pastel	Red
OPEN FLOWER				
Bowl, 9"	$35.00	$45.00		

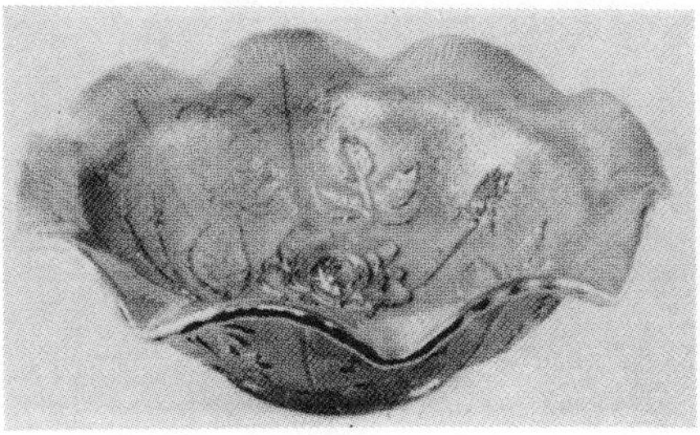

OPEN ROSE				
Bowl, 10"	$40.00	$50.00	$ 75.00	
Bowl, 5"	20.00	30.00	35.00	
Bowl, squat, 8"	35.00	45.00		
Footed bowl	35.00	45.00		
Plate, 9"	55.00	70.00	100.00	

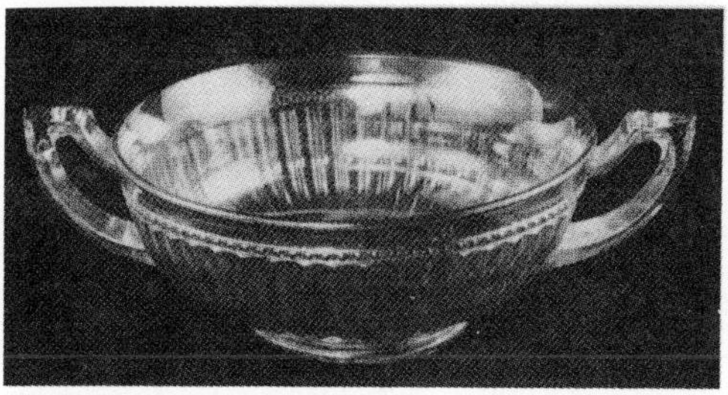

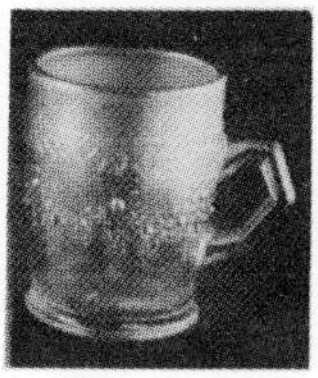

OPTIC AND BUTTONS				
Bowl, handled, 12"	$45.00			
Goblet	30.00			
Salt dish	30.00			
Plate	30.00			
ORANGE PEEL				
Punch bowl	$250.00			
Punch cup	25.00			
Small bowl	45.00			

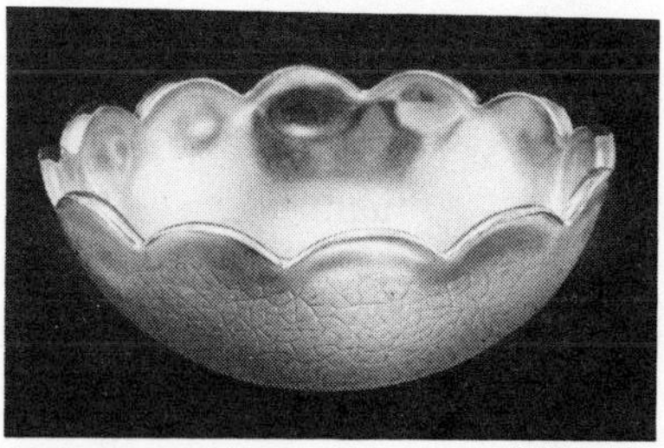

Pattern	Marigold	Green, Blue, Amethyst, Purple	Pastel	Red

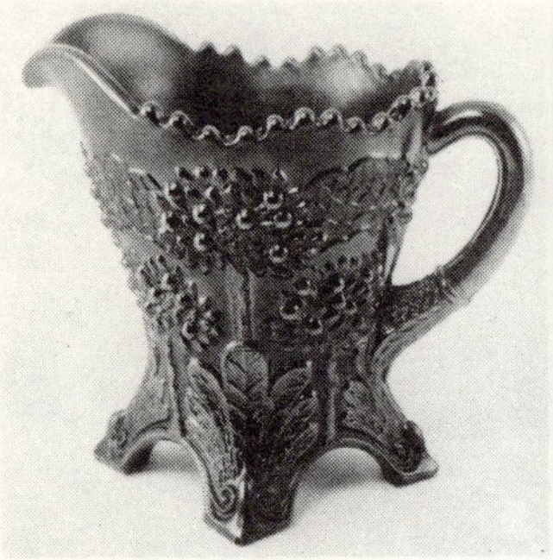 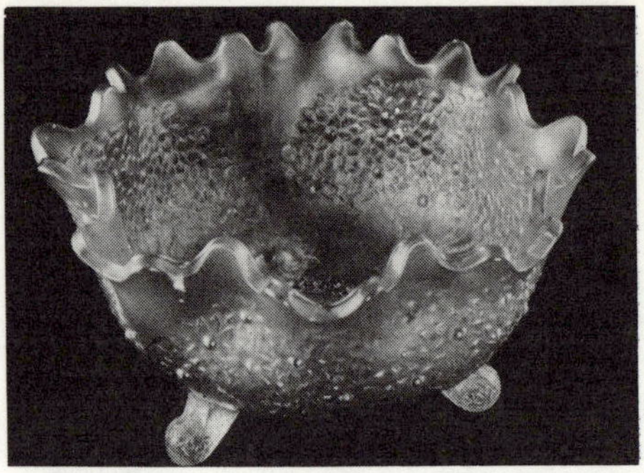

Pattern	Marigold	Green, Blue, Amethyst, Purple	Pastel	Red
ORANGE TREE				
Bowl, 9"	$ 45.00	$ 65.00	$100.00 (white)	
Bowl, 5"	30.00	35.00	50.00	
Hatpin holder	175.00	200.00		
Mug	40.00	50.00		$225.00
Pitcher, small	50.00	60.00		
Powder jar, cover	65.00	75.00		
Punch bowl with base	175.00	250.00	500.00 (white)	
Punch cup	35.00	25.00	50.00	
Pitcher	200.00	275.00	650.00 (white)	
Tumbler	45.00	55.00	100.00	
Centerpiece bowl, footed		600.00		
Plate, 9"	100.00	150.00	150.00	
Wineglass	40.00	50.00		
ORANGE TREE ORCHARD				
Pitcher	$225.00	$250.00	$500.00 (white)	
Tumbler	50.00	75.00	100.00	
ORIENTAL POPPY				
Pitcher	$300.00	$425.00	$850.00 (ice blue)	
Tumbler	55.00	75.00	100.00	
OVAL AND ROUND				
Bowl, 9"	$25.00	$40.00		
Plate, 10"	45.00	75.00		

Pattern	Marigold	Green, Blue, Amethyst, Purple	Pastel	Red
OVAL STAR AND FAN				
Rose bowl	$60.00	$75.00		
PALM BEACH				
Bowl, 9"	$ 60.00		$100.00	
Bowl, 5"	35.00		40.00	
Butter dish with cover	145.00		250.00	
Creamer	45.00		75.00	
Sugar bowl	50.00		85.00	
Spooner	45.00		75.00	
Plate, 9"	125.00	$200.00		
Rose bowl	55.00	100.00		
Pitcher	200.00		500.00	
Tumbler	45.00		100.00	

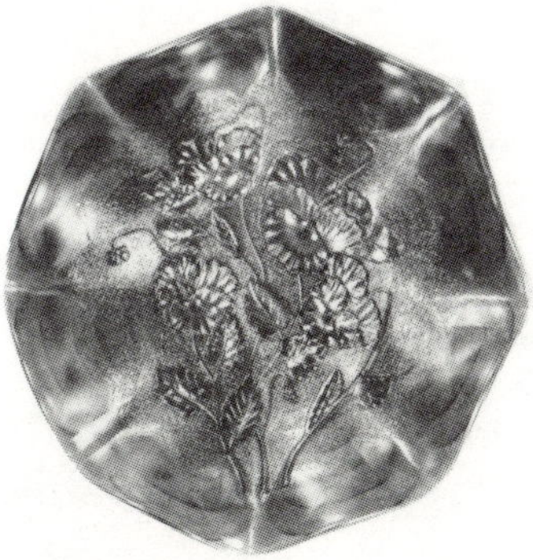

PANSY				
Bowl, 9"	$35.00	$45.00		
Creamer	30.00	40.00		
Sugar bowl	35.00	45.00		
Dresser tray	60.00	85.00		
Relish dish	30.00	40.00		
PEACH (NORTHWOOD)				
Bowl, 10"			$150.00 (white)	
Bowl, 5"			55.00	
Butter dish with cover		$200.00	250.00	
Creamer		100.00	100.00	
Sugar bowl		110.00	125.00	
Spooner		100.00	100.00	
Pitcher		500.00	550.00	
Tumbler		75.00	85.00	

Pattern,	Marigold	Green, Blue, Amethyst, Purple	Pastel	Red

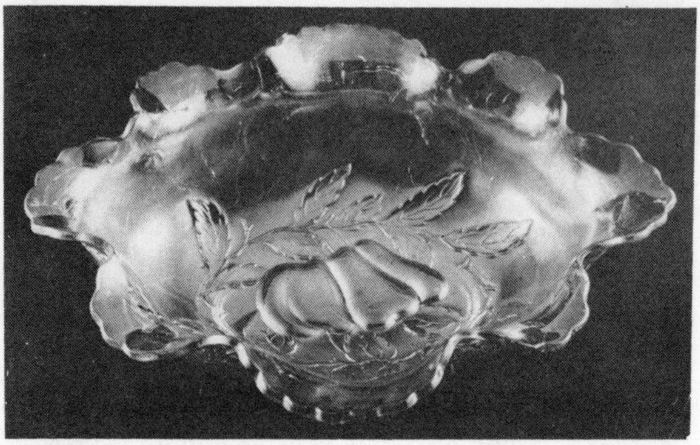

PEACH AND PEAR				
Oval bowl	$60.00	$125.00	$175.00	
PEACOCK				
Lamp base	$300.00	$350.00		$700.00
Vase	60.00	100.00		
PEACOCK AND DAHLIA				
Bowl, 9"	$40.00	$ 50.00		
Plate, 9"		225.00		

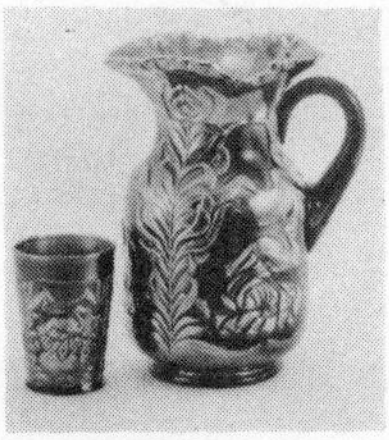

PEACOCK, FLUFFY				
Pitcher	$375.00	$950.00		
Tumbler	75.00	125.00		
PEACOCK AND GRAPE				
Bowl	$50.00	$65.00		$400.00

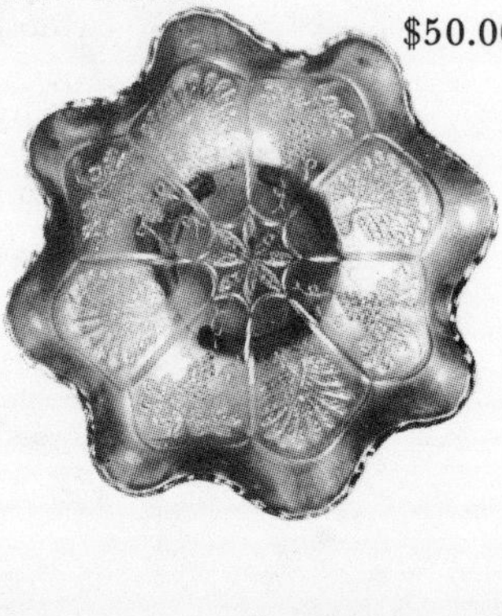

Pattern	Marigold	Green, Blue, Amethyst, Purple	Pastel	Red
PEACOCK AND URN				
Compote, large	$ 55.00	$100.00	$150.00	
Bowl, 9"	150.00	220.00	300.00 (ice blue) 4,000.00 (aqua (opales- cent) 750.00 (ice green)	
Bowl, 5"	55.00	75.00	125.00	
Plate, 9"	150.00	225.00		

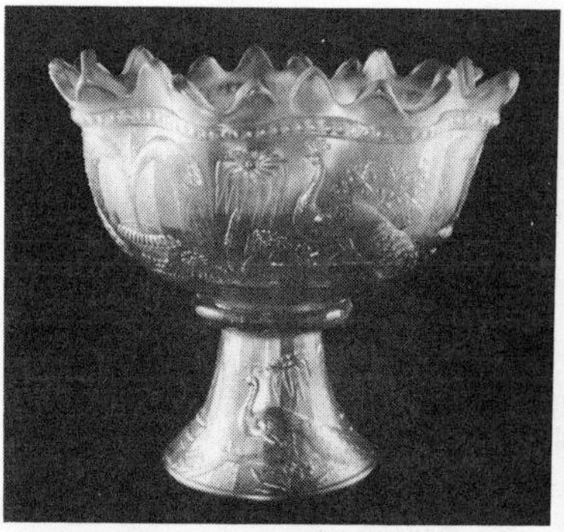

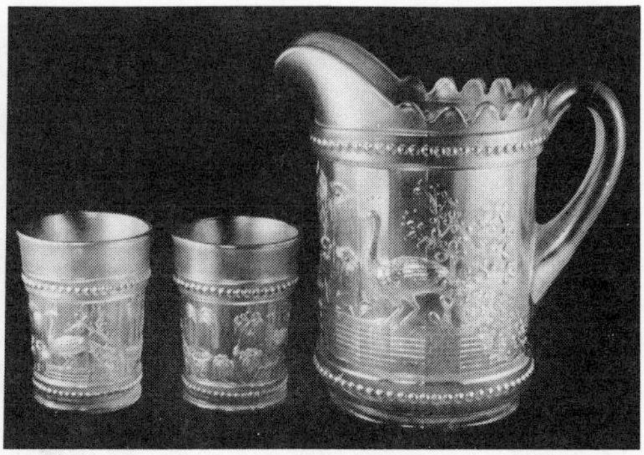

Pattern	Marigold	Green, Blue, Amethyst, Purple	Pastel	Red
PEACOCK AT THE FOUNTAIN				
Bowl, 9"	$ 75.00	$125.00	$225.00 (ice blue)	
Bowl, 5"	35.00	50.00	75.00	
Compote	160.00	250.00		
Butter dish with cover	150.00	200.00	300.00	
Creamer	55.00	85.00	140.00	
Sugar bowl	70.00	95.00	150.00	
Spooner	55.00	75.00	135.00	
Orange bowl	200.00	300.00	400.00	
Punch bowl with stand	200.00	300.00	425.00	
Punch cup	35.00	45.00	130.00	
Pitcher	200.00	275.00	600.00	
Tumbler	35.00	55.00	95.00	

Pattern	Marigold	Green, Blue, Amethyst, Purple	Pastel	Red
PEACOCK (MILLERSBURG)				
Bowl, 8"	$65.00	$ 150.00		
Plate, 11"		1,000.00		
PEACOCK, STRUTTING				
Creamer		$55.00		
Sugar bowl		65.00		
PEACOCK TAIL				
Bowl, 9"	$30.00	$40.00		
Bonbon	25.00	30.00		
Compote	20.00	30.00		
Hat	20.00	25.00		

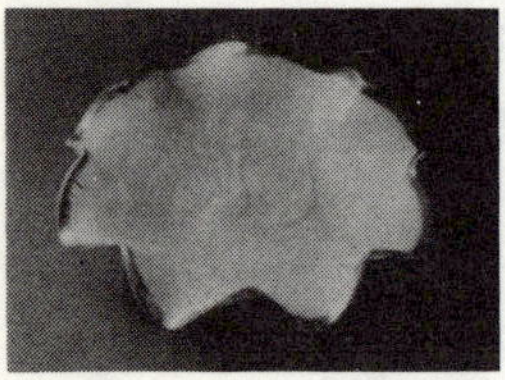

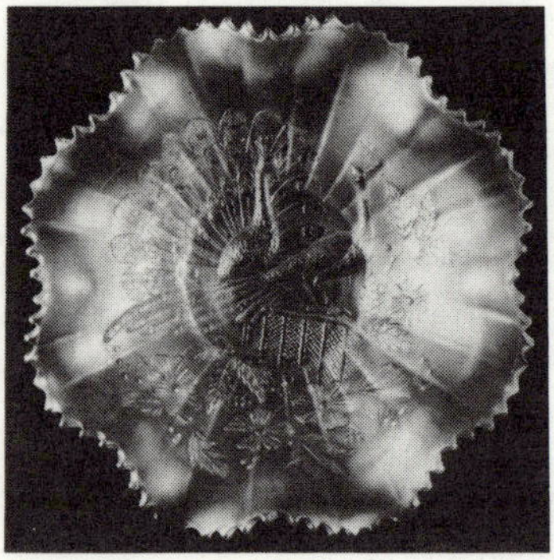

Pattern	Marigold	Green, Blue, Amethyst, Purple	Pastel	Red
PEACOCKS ON THE FENCE				
Bowl, 9"	$ 55.00	$ 75.00	$100.00	
			750.00 (white, gold rim)	
Plate, 9"	125.00	200.00	250.00 (ice blue)	
			200.00 (ice green)	
PEBBLE AND FAN				
Vase	$125.00	$125.00		
PEOPLE'S VASE	$6,000.00	$7,500.00		

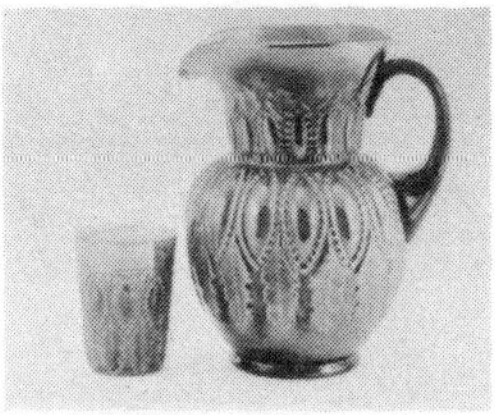

Pattern	Marigold	Green, Blue, Amethyst, Purple	Pastel	Red
PERFECTION				
Pitcher	$3,250.00	$3,250.00		
Tumbler	250.00	400.00		

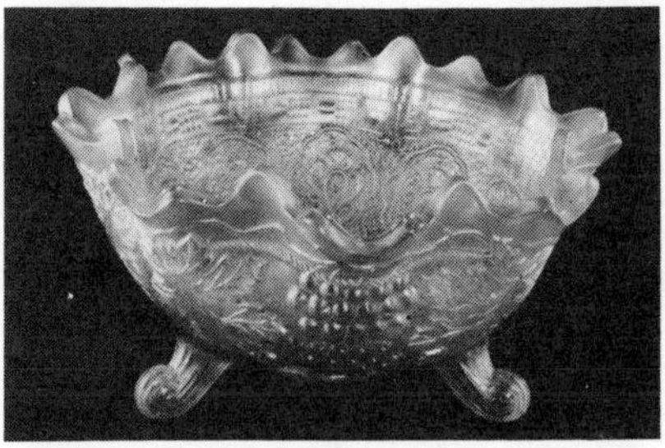

Pattern	Marigold	Green, Blue, Amethyst, Purple	Pastel	Red
PERSIAN GARDEN				
Bowl, 12"			$250.00 (white)	
Bowl, 5"			100.00	
Plate, 12"	$300.00	$ 900.00 4,500.00 (purple)	875.00 (peach opalescent)	
Fruit bowl with stand	225.00	325.00	450.00	
Plate, 7"	60.00	85.00	115.00	
PERSIAN MEDALLION				
Bonbon with handles	$30.00	$ 40.00	$145.00	
Bowl, 10"	50.00	70.00		$125.00
Compote	35.00	50.00		
Hair receiver	65.00	85.00		
Plate, 9"	65.00	125.00	225.00	
Rose bowl	55.00	75.00	115.00	
PETALS				
Bowl, 9"	$30.00	$40.00	$ 85.00	
Compote	25.00	35.00	100.00	

Pattern	Marigold	Green, Blue, Amethyst, Purple	Pastel	Red
PETAL AND FAN				
Bowl, 10"	$35.00	$55.00	$60.00 (peach opalescent)	
Bowl, 5"	20.00	25.00	25.00	
PETER RABBIT				
Bowl, 9"	$ 750.00	$1,500.00		
Plate, 9"	1,500.00	2,000.00		
PILLOW AND SUNBURST				
Bowl, 8"	$ 30.00	$ 60.00		
Wine decanter	125.00	500.00		
Wineglasses, stemmed	35.00	100.00		
PINEAPPLE				
Bowl, footed, 8"	$60.00	$75.00		
Compote		70.00		
Creamer	40.00	45.00		
PINE CONE				
Bowl, 6"	$35.00	$ 50.00		
Plate, 8"	75.00	150.00		
Plate, 6"	40.00	55.00		
Bonbon	30.00	45.00		
PINWHEEL				
Bowl, 6"	$30.00			
Plate, 6"	40.00			
PIPE HUMIDOR (MILLERSBURG)	$3,000.00	$5,000.00		
PLAID				
Bowl, 9"	$30.00	$50.00		$250.00
Plate, 9"	65.00	95.00		
POINSETTIA AND LATTICE				
Bowl, 8"	$75.00	$100.00		
POND LILY				
Bonbon	$25.00	$35.00	$95.00	

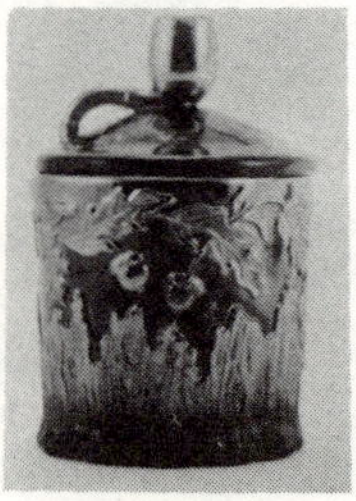

Pattern	Marigold	Green, Blue, Amethyst, Purple	Pastel	Red

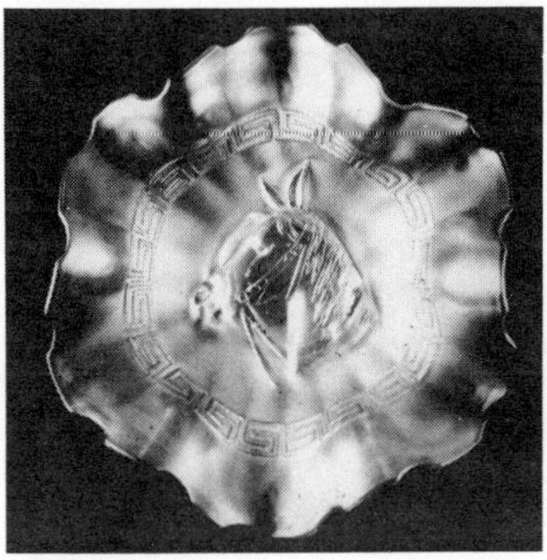

Pattern	Marigold	Green, Blue, Amethyst, Purple	Pastel	Red
PONY				
Bowl, 8"	$100.00	$150.00	$250.00 (ice green)	
Plate	200.00	300.00		
POPPY (MILLERSBURG)				
Compote		$200.00		

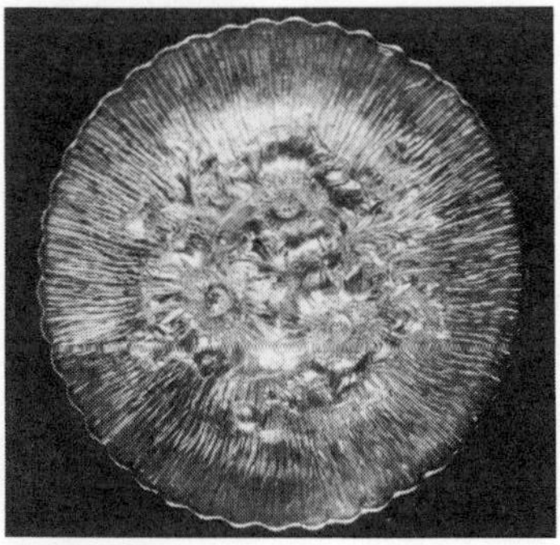

Pattern	Marigold	Green, Blue, Amethyst, Purple	Pastel	Red
POPPY SHOW				
Bowl, 9"	$150.00	$275.00	$175.00	
Plate, 9"	250.00	400.00	450.00 (ice blue)	
Vase, 12"	350.00	600.00		
POWDER JAR (figure on cover)	$35.00			

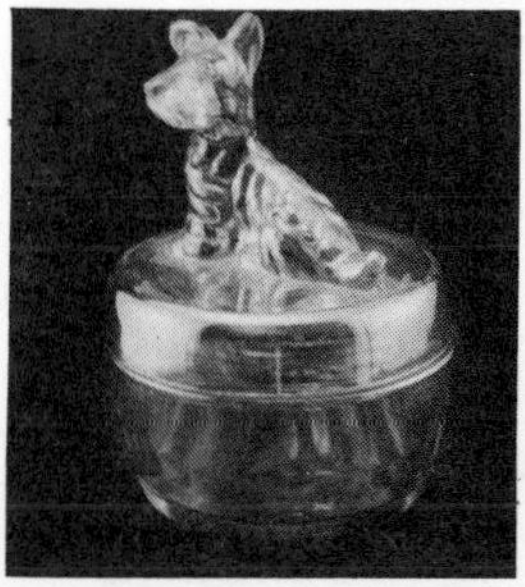

Pattern	Marigold	*Green, Blue, Amethyst, Purple*	Pastel	Red
PRAYER RUG				
Bonbon			$100.00 (peach opalescent)	
PRETTY PANELS				
Pitcher		$500.00		
Tumbler		85.00		
PRIMROSE				
Bowl, 9"-10"	$40.00	$75.00		
PRINCELY PLUMES				
Hatpin		$45.00		
PRINCESS				
Lamp		$850.00		
PROPELLER				
Candy dish, footed	$30.00			
PUZZLE				
Bonbon	$30.00	$40.00	$45.00	
Compote	35.00	45.00	50.00	
QUEEN'S LAMP		$750.00		
QUESTION MARKS				
Bonbon	$30.00	$40.00	$50.00	
Compote	25.00	35.00	60.00	
QUILL				
Pitcher	$400.00	$900.00		
Tumbler	100.00	150.00		
RAGGED ROBIN				
Bowl, 9"	$45.00	$55.00	$75.00	

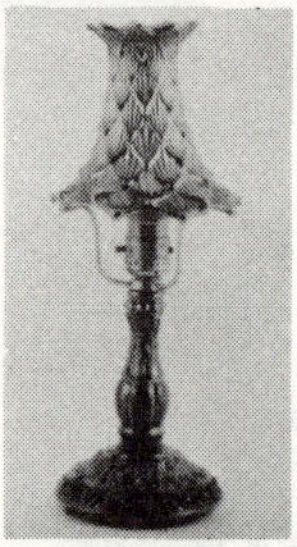

Pattern	Marigold	*Green, Blue, Amethyst, Purple*	Pastel	Red
RAINDROPS				
Bowl, 8"		$60.00	$100.00 (peach opalescent)	
Bowl, 10"		75.00	125.00	

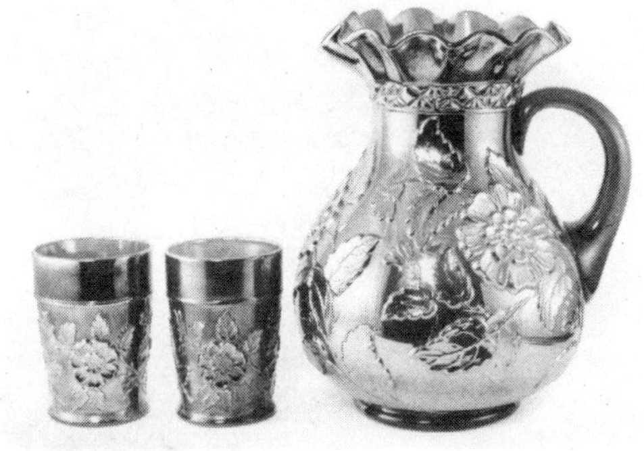

Pattern	Marigold	*Green, Blue, Amethyst, Purple*	Pastel	Red
RAMBLER ROSE				
Pitcher	$175.00	$300.00		
Tumbler	35.00	50.00		
RANGER				
Pitcher	$125.00	$175.00		
Tumbler	40.00	50.00		
RASPBERRY (NORTHWOOD)				
Bowl, 9"	$ 55.00	$ 75.00		
Bowl, 5"	30.00	40.00		
Milk pitcher	100.00	250.00	$900.00 (ice green)	
Sauceboat	50.00	70.00		
Pitcher	200.00	350.00	600.00 (ice blue)	
Tumbler	30.00	50.00	100.00	
Compote	50.00	65.00		
RAYS AND RIBBONS				
Bowl	$30.00	$40.00		
REGAL IRIS				
Gone-with-the-wind lamp	$1,500.00			$4,000.00

Pattern	Marigold	Green, Blue, Amethyst, Purple	Pastel	Red
RIB AND PANEL				
Cuspidor	$125.00			
Vase	55.00			
RIB AND SWIRL				
Lampshade			$375.00	
RIBBON BLOCK				
Lamp	$800.00			
RIPPLE				
Funeral vase, 8"-20"	$ 35.00	$ 50.00		
	150.00	300.00		
ROCK CRYSTAL				
Punch bowl with stand		$800.00		
Punch cup		65.00		
ROBIN				
Mug	$ 50.00			
Pitcher	225.00			
Tumbler	55.00			
ROOSTER HATPIN	$25.00	$35.00		$25.00
ROSALIND				
Bowl	$30.00			
ROSE GARDEN				
Milk pitcher	$400.00	$600.00		
Vase		225.00		
ROSE PANELS				
Compote, large	$75.00			
ROSE PILLARS				
Vase	$90.00	$ 90.00		
		400.00 (green)		
ROSE SHOW				
Bowl, 9"	$200.00	$250.00	$300.00	
Plate, 9"	300.00	400.00	400.00	

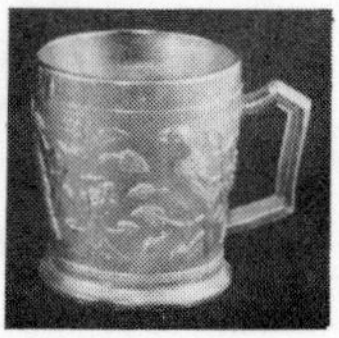

Pattern	Marigold	*Green, Blue, Amethyst, Purple*	Pastel	Red
ROSE SPRAY				
Compote			$85.00	
ROSE TREE				
Bowl		$80.00		
ROSES AND RUFFLES				
Gone-with-the-wind lamp	$2,000.00			$4,000.00
ROSETTE				
Bowl	$30.00	$40.00		
ROUND-UP				
Bowl, 9"	$ 50.00	$ 60.00	$100.00	
Plate, 9"	125.00	150.00	200.00 (peach opalescent)	
RUFFLED RIB				
Vase	$30.00	$40.00		
S-BAND				
Compote		$50.00		
S-REPEAT				
Creamer		$ 80.00		
Punch bowl with stand		1,000.00		
Punch cup		40.00		
Toothpick holder		225.00		
SAILBOATS				
Bowl, 7"	$35.00	$45.00		
Compote	40.00			
Goblet	50.00	65.00		
Wineglass, stemmed	35.00	45.00		
SAILING SHIP				
Plate, 8"	$35.00			
SCALE BAND				
Bowl, 8"	$ 35.00			
Pitcher	100.00	$125.00		
Tumbler	25.00	35.00		

Pattern	Marigold	Green, Blue, Amethyst, Purple	Pastel	Red
SCALES				
Bowl, 8"-9"	$40.00	$30.00	$50.00	
Plate, 7"	45.00	55.00	75.00 (peach opalescent)	
SCROLL				
Pin tray	$45.00			
SCROLL EMBOSSED				
Bowl, 9"	$30.00	$ 50.00		
Plate, 9"	50.00	100.00	$115.00	
SCOTCH THISTLE				
Compote	$30.00	$50.00		
SEACOAST				
Pin tray	$300.00	$400.00		
SEA GULL				
Bowl	$70.00			
SEAWEED				
Bowl	$ 30.00	$40.00	$65.00	
Lamp	200.00			
SHELL AND JEWEL				
Creamer	$55.00	$70.00		
Sugar bowl	60.00	75.00		
SHELL CARNIVAL				
Bowl, 9"	$ 30.00	$ 45.00		
Compote	30.00			
Plate, 8"	100.00	125.00		
SHIP AND STARS				
Plate	$40.00			

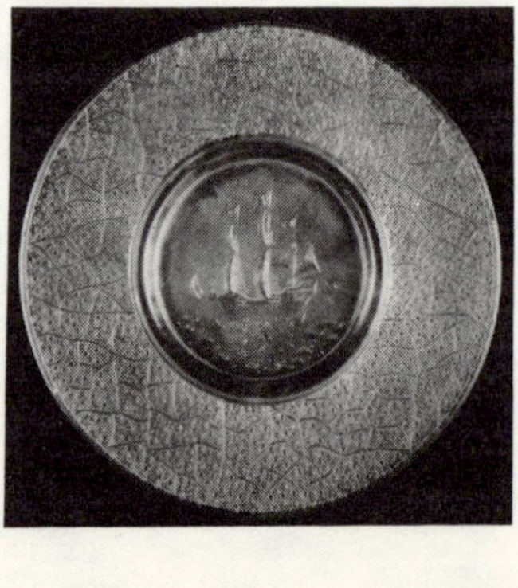

Pattern	Marigold	*Green, Blue, Amethyst, Purple*	Pastel	Red
SHRINE				
Toothpick holder			$225.00	

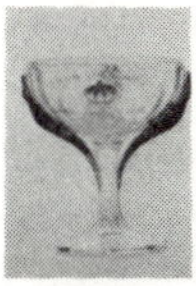
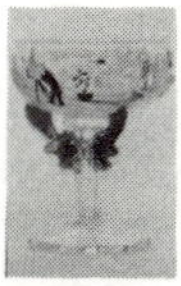
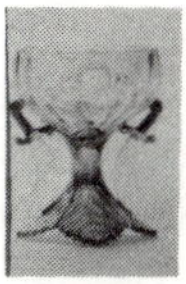

Pattern	Marigold	Green, Blue, Amethyst, Purple	Pastel	Red
SHRINER SOUVENIR CHAMPAGNE GLASSES				
Louisville			$125.00 (clambroth, clear)	
New Orleans			125.00	
Rochester			200.00	
SINGLE FLOWER				
Bowl, 8"	$35.00	$55.00		
SINGLE FLOWER, FRAMED				
Bowl, 8"	$40.00	$50.00		

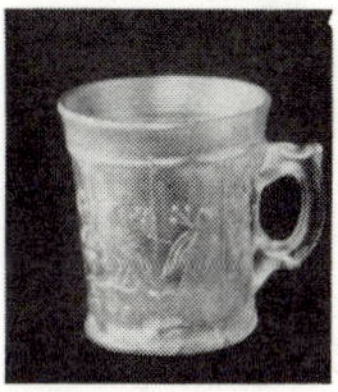
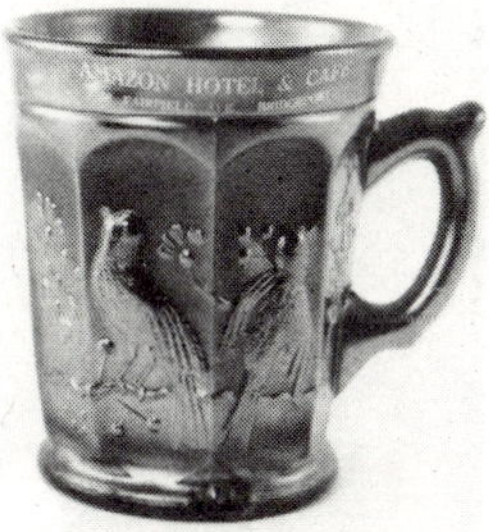

Pattern	Marigold	Green, Blue, Amethyst, Purple	Pastel	Red
SINGING BIRDS				
Bowl, 10"	$ 50.00	$100.00		
Bowl, 5"	25.00	35.00		
Butter dish	200.00	275.00		
Creamer	65.00	115.00		
Sugar bowl	75.00	125.00		
Spooner	65.00	115.00		
Mug	55.00	70.00		
Pitcher	225.00	375.00		
Tumbler	50.00	75.00		
Advertising mug	100.00	125.00		

Pattern	*Marigold*	*Green, Blue, Amethyst, Purple*	*Pastel*	*Red*
SIX PETALS				
Bowl	$30.00	$40.00	$ 85.00	
Plate			225.00	
SKI STAR				
Bowl, 10"	$50.00	$75.00	$125.00 (peach opalescent)	
Bowl, 6"	40.00	50.00	75.00	
Handled basket			150.00	
SODA GOLD				
Candlesticks (pair)	$ 35.00			
Pitcher	145.00	$160.00		
Tumbler	20.00	35.00		
Vase	50.00			
Spittoon	40.00	50.00		

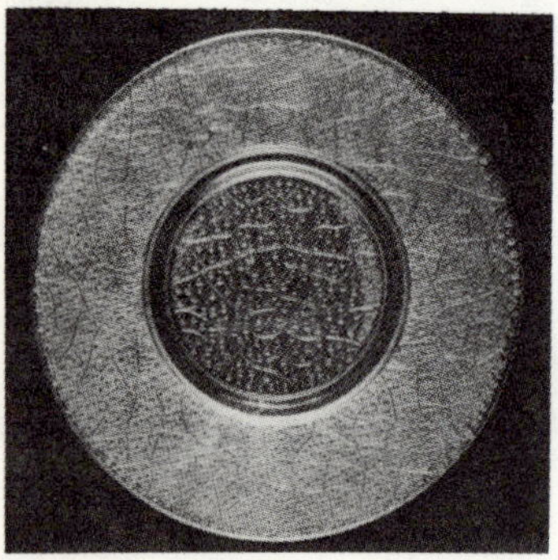

SODA GOLD SPEARS				
Plate	$20.00			
SOLDIERS AND SAILORS				
Plate	$450.00	$550.00		
SOUTACHE				
Bowl, footed, 9"			$ 75.00 (peach opalescent)	
Plate			200.00 (peach opalescent)	

Pattern	Marigold	Green, Blue, Amethyst, Purple	Pastel	Red

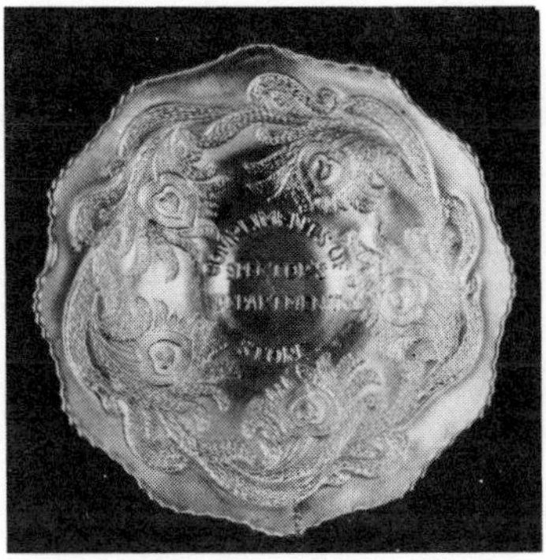

Pattern	Marigold	Green, Blue, Amethyst, Purple	Pastel	Red
SPECTOR'S PLATE	$250.00			

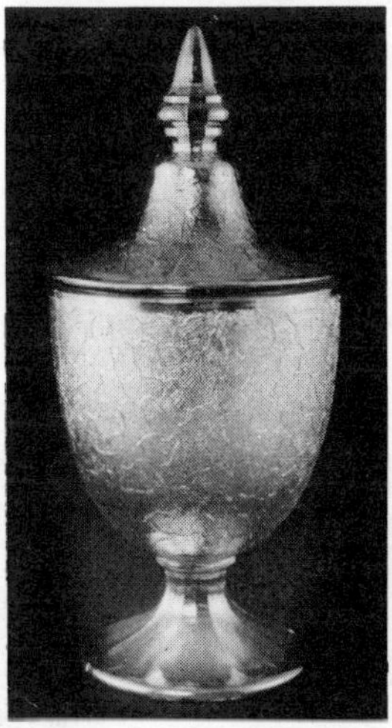

Pattern	Marigold	Green, Blue, Amethyst, Purple	Pastel	Red
SPIDER WEB AND SODA GOLD				
Pitcher	$175.00			
Tumbler	30.00			
Candy dish	30.00			
SPHINX PAPERWEIGHT	$500.00			
SPRING OPENING PLATE		$250.00		
SPRINGTIME				
Bowl, 9"	$ 50.00	$100.00		
Bowl, 5"	30.00	40.00		
Butter dish	175.00	250.00		
Creamer	60.00	100.00		
Sugar bowl	70.00	110.00		
Spooner	60.00	100.00		
Pitcher	350.00	450.00	$550.00	
Tumbler	60.00	85.00	110.00	

Pattern	Marigold	Green, Blue, Amethyst, Purple	Pastel	Red

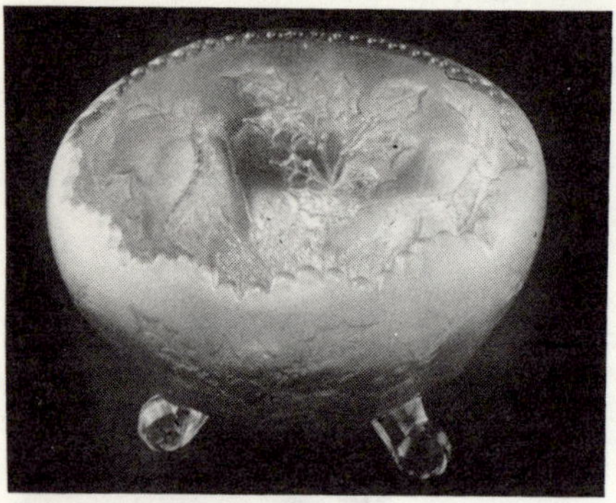

STAG AND HOLLY				
Bowl, footed, 11"	$750.00	$250.00		
Chop plate, footed	350.00	450.00		
Large rose bowl	250.00	375.00		
Plate, 7"	300.00			

STAR AND FAN				
Vase		$90.00		

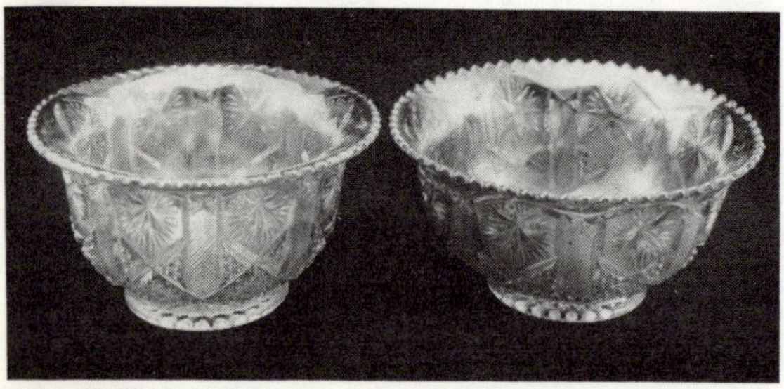

STAR AND FILE				
Bowl, 9"	$ 40.00			
Bowl, 5"	15.00			
Creamer	17.50			
Sugar bowl	17.50			
Pitcher	250.00			
Tumbler	65.00			

STAR CENTER				
Bowl, 9"	$30.00	$40.00	$60.00	
Plate, 8"	50.00	60. 00	75.00	

Pattern	Marigold	Green, Blue, Amethyst, Purple	Pastel	Red
STAR FLOWER				
Pitcher	$350.00	$650.00		
Tumbler	75.00	150.00		

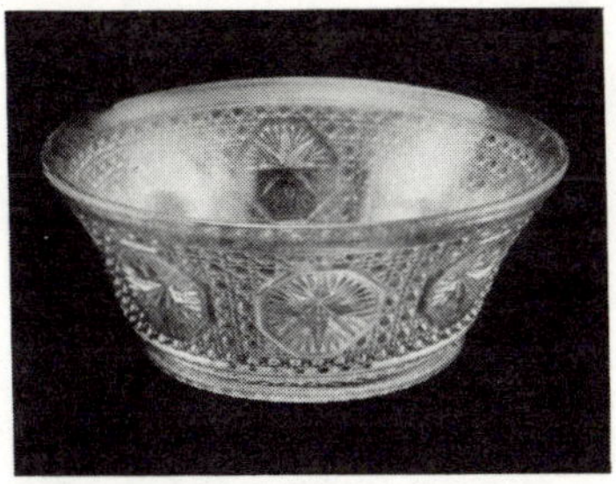

STAR MEDALLION				
Bowl, 9"	$30.00			
Bowl, 5"	15.00			
Milk pitcher	40.00	$100.00		
Plate, 9"	40.00			
Goblet	30.00			
Tumbler	40.00			
STAR OF DAVID				
Bowl, footed, 9"	$60.00	$100.00		
STARFLOWER				
Pitcher	$550.00	$675.00		
Tumbler	150.00	200.00		
Button		25.00		

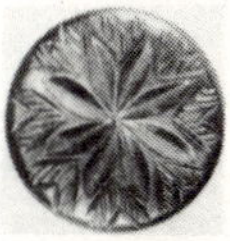

STIPPLED FLOWER				
Bowl, 9"	$45.00			

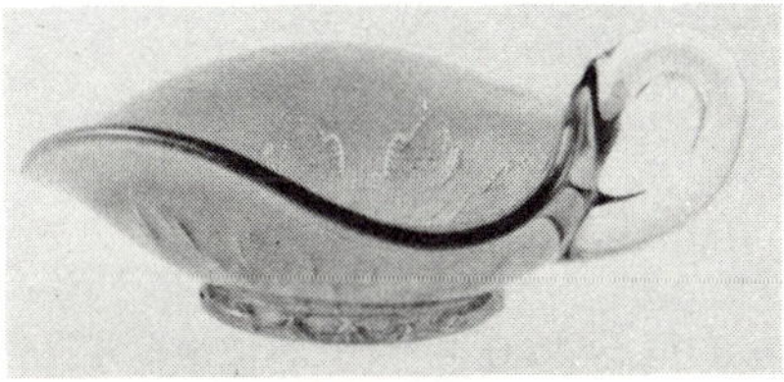

STIPPLED LEAVES				
Bonbon	$40.00			

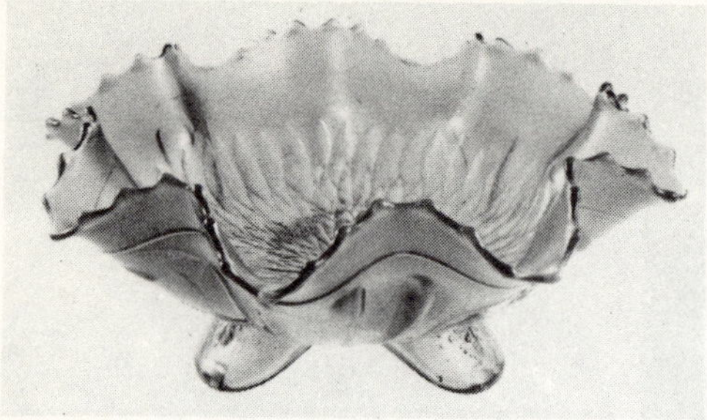

Pattern	Marigold	Green, Blue, Amethyst, Purple	Pastel	Red
STIPPLED PETALS				
Bowl		$50.00	$60.00 (peach opalescent)	
STIPPLED RAYS				
Bonbon	$30.00	$40.00		$150.00
Bowl, 9"	40.00	50.00		250.00
Compote	25.00	40.00		
Plate, 9"	40.00	50.00		300.00
STORK CHILD'S PLATE	$60.00			
STORK AND RUSHES				
Basket, handled	$ 85.00			
Bowl, 10"	40.00	$ 50.00		
Bowl, 5"	25.00	30.00		
Hat	40.00			
Mug	50.00	65.00		
Punch bowl with stand	200.00	250.00		
Punch cup	25.00	35.00		
Pitcher	150.00	350.00		
Tumbler	35.00	60.00		
STORK VASE	$65.00			
STRAWBERRY				
Bowl, 9"	$ 40.00	$ 60.00		
Bowl, 5"	20.00	25.00		
Epergne	250.00	300.00		
Plate, 6"	65.00	90.00		
Plate, 9"	75.00	100.00		

Pattern	Marigold	Green, Blue, Amethyst, Purple	Pastel	Red
STRAWBERRY (MILLERSBURG)				
Bowl, 8"	$60.00	$110.00		
Bowl, 5"	35.00	55.00		
Epergne		250.00		
Sauce boat			$100.00	
STRAWBERRY SCROLL				
Pitcher	$600.00	$2,000.00		
Tumbler	150.00	250.00		
STREAM OF HEARTS				
Compote	$45.00		$100.00	
STUDS				
Milk pitcher	$45.00			
Small tumbler	20.00			
Tray	50.00			
SUNFLOWER				
Bowl, footed, 7"	$ 30.00	$ 40.00		
Plate	200.00	250.00		
SUNFLOWER DIAMONDS				
Vase	$40.00	$65.00		

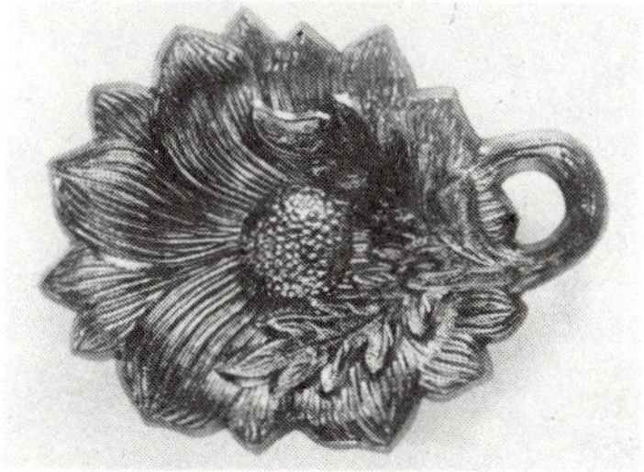

SUNFLOWER PINTRAY	$200.00	$250.00		
SUNGOLD				
Epergne	$150.00			
SUNKEN HOLLYHOCK				
Gone-with-the-wind lamp	$2,500.00			$5,000.00

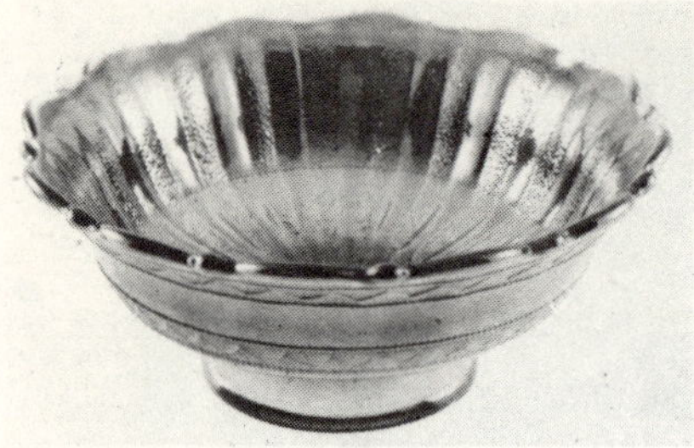

Pattern	Marigold	Green, Blue, Amethyst, Purple	Pastel	Red
SUNRAY				
Bowl	$35.00			

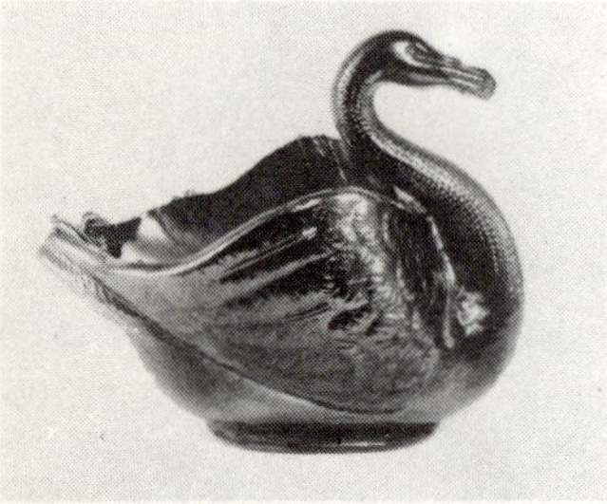

SWAN				
Pastel color or dark (beware reproductions)	$30.00	$250.00	$250.00 (peach opalescent)	
SWIRL				
Bowl, 7"	$20.00			
Epergne			$125.00 (peach opalescent)	
Plate, 9"	50.00	$65.00		
SWIRL HOBNAIL				
Rose bowl	$200.00	$350.00		
Spittoon	375.00	425.00		
Vase, 12"	65.00	95.00		
Vase, 20"	225.00	275.00		
SWIRL RIB				
Pitcher	$135.00	$190.00		
Tumbler	40.00	55.00		
Vase	30.00	50.00		

Pattern	Marigold	Green, Blue, Amethyst, Purple	Pastel	Red
TEN MUMS				
Bowl, 9"	$ 65.00	$100.00		
Plate, 10"	150.00	250.00		
Pitcher	300.00	550.00		
Tumbler	65.00	100.00		
THISTLE AND LOTUS				
Bowl, 8"	$25.00	$45.00		
THISTLE AND THORN				
Bowl, footed, 6"	$ 40.00			
Creamer	40.00			
Plate, 6"	45.00	$100.00		
Plate, 9"	125.00	250.00		
THISTLE (FENTON)				
Banana boat	$100.00	$175.00		
THREE FRUITS				
Bonbon, footed	$35.00	$ 50.00	$150.00 (aqua opalescent)	
Bowl, 9"	50.00	50.00		
Plate, 9"	75.00	125.00	250.00	
THREE-IN-ONE				
Bowl, 8"	$35.00	$50.00		
Bowl, 4"	20.00	35.00		
THUMBPRINT AND OVAL				
Vase, smooth glass	$ 90.00	$125.00		
Vase, ribbed	125.00	140.00	$250.00	

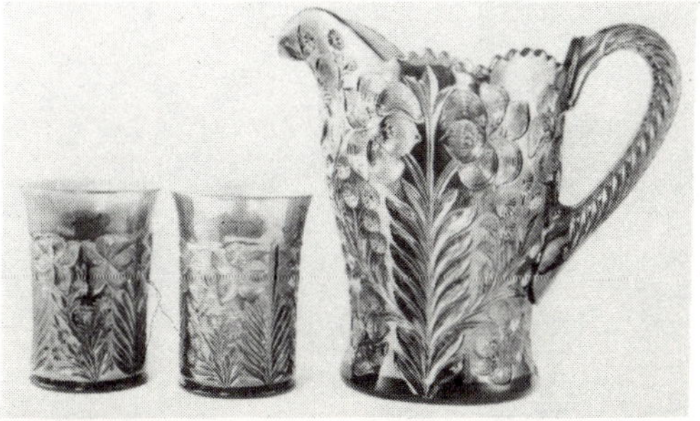

Pattern	Marigold	Green, Blue, Amethyst, Purple	Pastel	Red
TIGER LILY				
Pitcher	$250.00	$300.00	(Pastels are	
Tumbler	60.00	70.00	(reproductions)	

Pattern	Marigold	Green, Blue, Amethyst, Purple	Pastel	Red
TORNADO				
Vase	$250.00	$275.00		

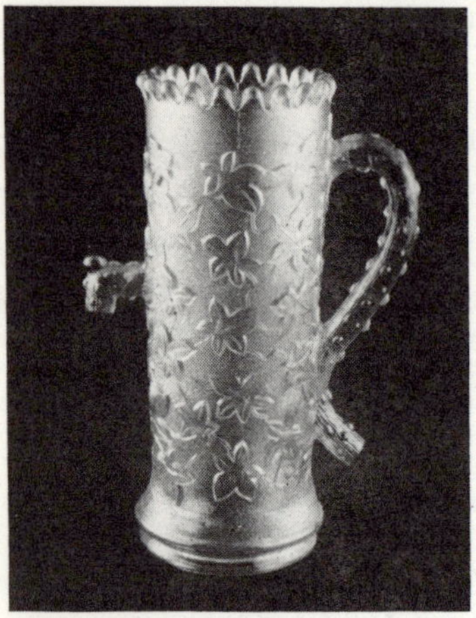

TOWN PUMP	$700.00	$575.00		

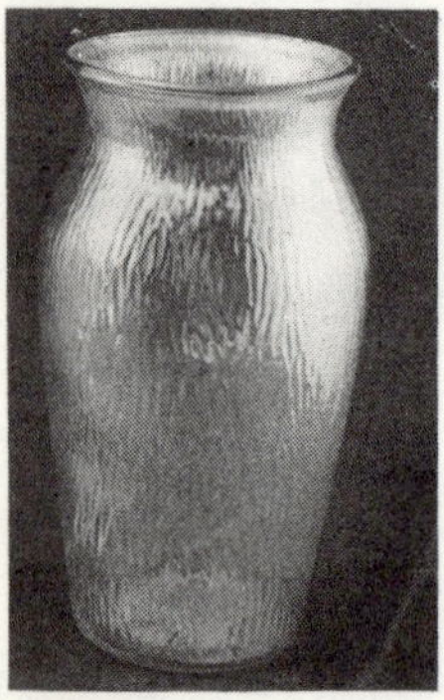

TREE BARK				
Pitcher	$65.00			
Tumbler	25.00			
Vase	35.00			
TREE TRUNK				
Vase, 12"	$ 25.00	$ 35.00	$ 90.00	
Vase, 20"	125.00	250.00	300.00	

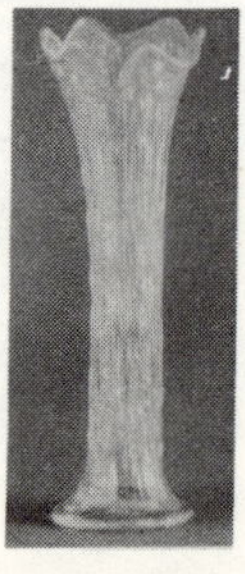

Pattern	Marigold	Green, Blue, Amethyst, Purple	Pastel	Red
TRIPLETS				
Bowl, 8"	$25.00	$40.00		
Hat shape	25.00	35.00		
TULIP AND CANE				
Goblet	$55.00			

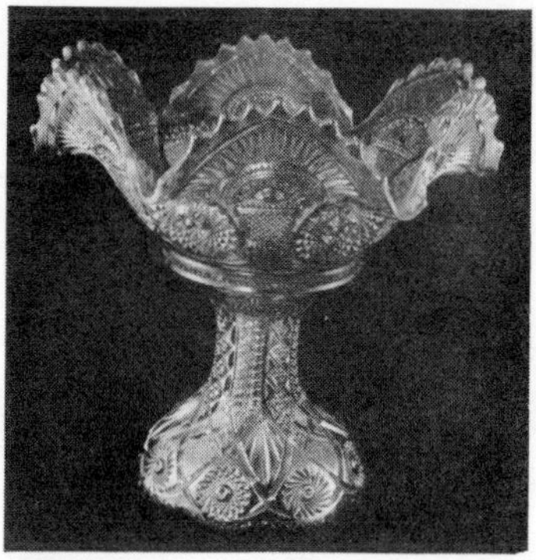

Pattern	Marigold	Green, Blue, Amethyst, Purple	Pastel	Red
TWINS				
Bowl, 9"	$ 45.00			
Bowl, 5"	20.00			
Bowl, 10"	45.00	$65.00		
Centerpiece fruit bowl	125.00			
Punch bowl with stand	125.00			

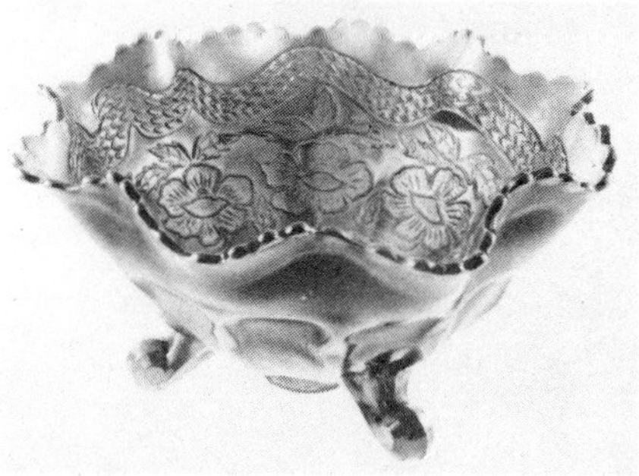

Pattern	Marigold	Green, Blue, Amethyst, Purple	Pastel	Red
TWO FLOWERS				
Bonbon	$25.00	$35.00	$ 50.00	
Bowl, footed, 10"	45.00	90.00	110.00	
Bowl, footed, 7"	35.00	55.00	65.00	

Pattern	Marigold	*Green, Blue, Amethyst, Purple*	Pastel	Red
TWO FRUITS				
Bowl, oval	$ 65.00	$115.00		
Bride's basket	175.00	290.00		
VENETIAN				
Giant rose bowl	$ 850.00	$1,250.00		
Lamp with shade (if found)	3,000.00	5,000.00		
VICTORIAN				
Bowl, 11"		$150.00		

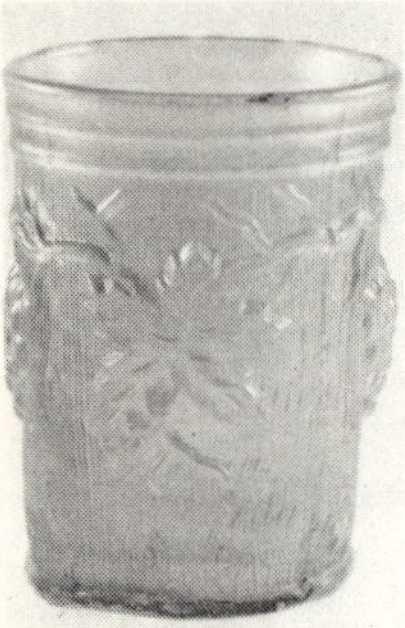

Pattern	Marigold	*Green, Blue, Amethyst, Purple*	Pastel	Red
VINEYARD				
Pitcher	$150.00	$400.00		
Tumbler	50.00	90.00		
VINING TWIGS				
Bowl, 8"	$40.00	$50.00		
Hat shape	30.00	45.00		

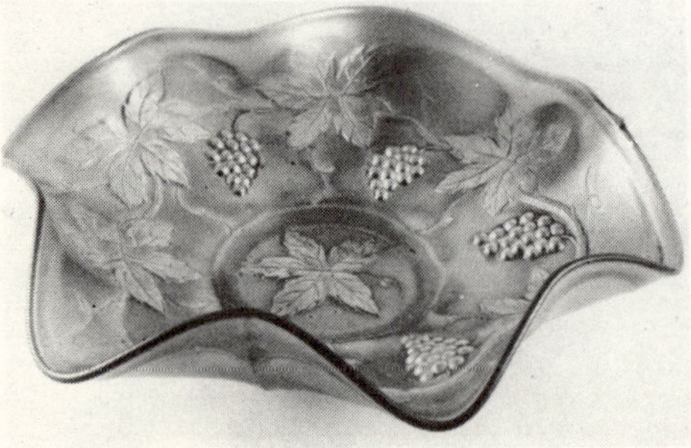

Pattern	Marigold	*Green, Blue, Amethyst, Purple*	Pastel	Red
VINTAGE				
Dresser tray, oval	$125.00		$150.00	
Epergne	165.00	$185.00		

Pattern	Marigold	Green, Blue, Amethyst, Purple	Pastel	Red
Nut dish (Little Fernery)	$55.00	$ 55.00	$125.00	$250.00
Powder jar	55.00			
Sandwich tray	35.00	40.00		
Wine bottle	65.00	175.00		
Wineglass	25.00	20.00		
VINTAGE (MILLERSBURG)				
Bowl, 9"		$100.00		
VINTAGE BANDED				
Mug	$ 50.00			
Water pitcher	275.00			

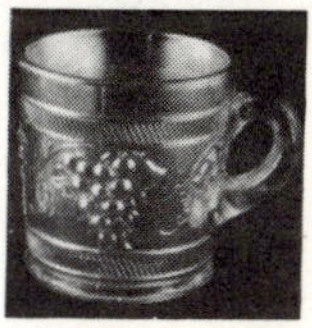

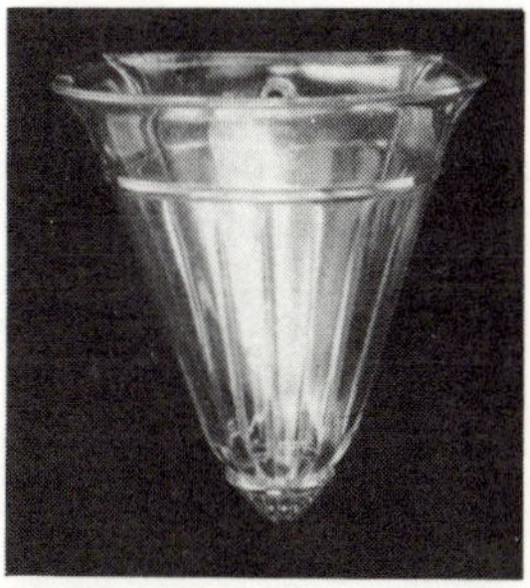

Pattern	Marigold	Green, Blue, Amethyst, Purple	Pastel	Red
WALL POCKET (vase)	$50.00			
WAFFLE BLOCK				
Basket	$ 35.00		$ 75.00	
Punch bowl with stand	150.00			
Punch cup	30.00			
Pitcher	150.00			
Tumbler	40.00			
Vase	35.00		65.00	
WATERLILY AND DRAGONFLY				
Bowl, 10"	$65.00			
WESTERN DAISY				
Bowl, 8"	$30.00	$40.00		
Hat	20.00	35.00		

Pattern	*Marigold*	*Green, Blue, Amethyst Purple*	*Pastel*	*Red*
WHIRLING LEAVES				
Bowl, 9"	$ 60.00	$ 90.00		
Plate, 9"	125.00	175.00	$300.00	
WHIRLING STAR				
Bowl, 9"	$35.00			
Compote	55.00			
WHITE OAK				
Pitcher	$450.00	$550.00		
Tumbler	75.00	110.00		
WIDE PANEL				
Plate, 15"	$125.00			
Compote	30.00			
Console bowl	100.00			
Candlesticks (pair)	45.00			
Epergne	525.00	$650.00	$2,225.00 (aqua opalescent)	
Goblet	35.00			

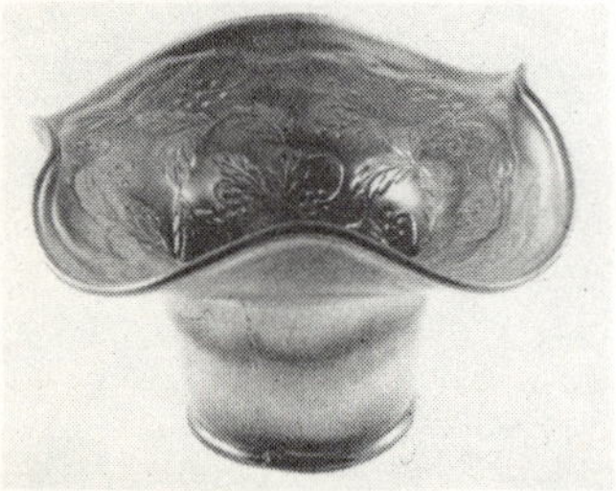

WILD BLACKBERRY				
Hat		$40.00		$100.00
Bowl		75.00		175.00
WILD ROSE				
Syrup pitcher	$350.00			
WILD ROSE (NORTHWOOD)				
Bowl, 8"	$ 35.00	$45.00	$ 65.00	
Bride's basket	175.00		275.00	

Pattern	Marigold	Green, Blue, Amethyst, Purple	Pastel	Red
WINDFLOWER				
Bowl, 9"	$35.00	$ 50.00		
Plate, 9"	65.00	100.00		
Sauceboat	45.00			

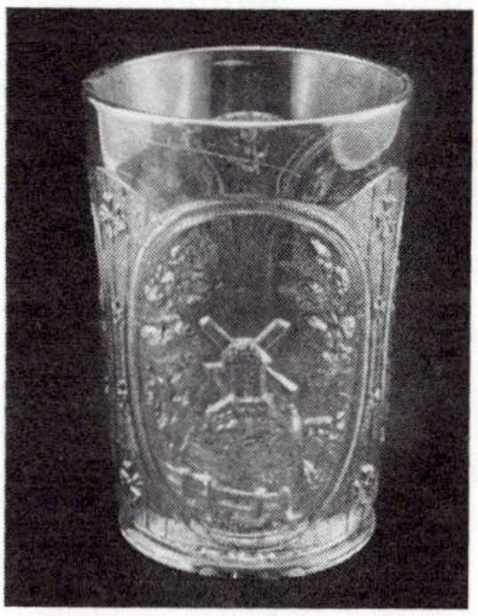

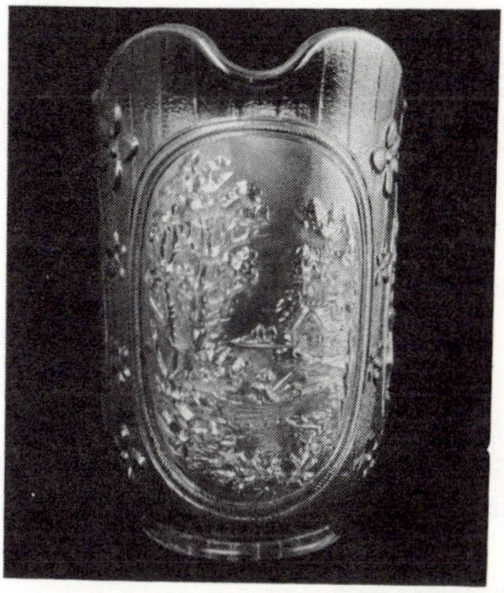

Pattern	Marigold	Green, Blue, Amethyst, Purple	Pastel	Red
WINDMILL				
Bowl, 8"	$ 25.00	$ 40.00		
Pitcher	125.00	250.00		
Tumbler	30.00	55.00		
Milk pitcher	145.00	200.00		
Pickle dish	30.00	45.00		
WINDMILL AND FLOWERS				
Dresser tray		$75.00		
WINDMILL AND MUMS				
Bowl, 10"	$50.00	$75.00		
WINE AND ROSES				
Pitcher	$150.00			
Wineglass	45.00			
WIDE OWL BANK (late)	$15.00			

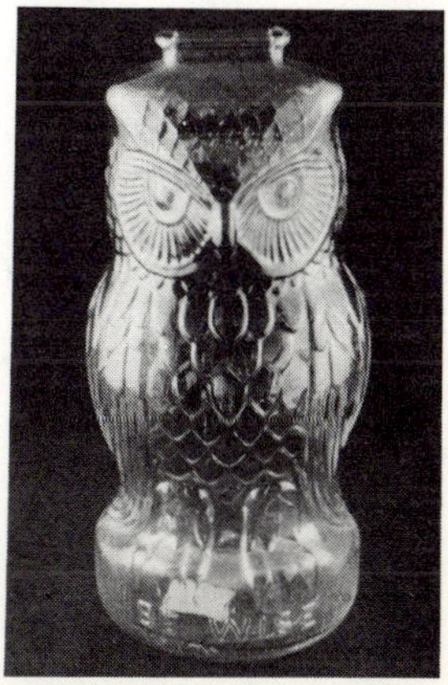

Pattern	Marigold	Green, Blue, Amethyst, Purple	Pastel	Red
WISHBONE				
Bowl, footed, 8"	$ 60.00	$ 85.00	$ 125.00	
Epergne	200.00	210.00	325.00	
Pitcher	550.00	1,000.00	1,500.00	
Tumbler	90.00	125.00	275.00	
Plate, 10"	140.00	250.00	300.00	
WISHBONE AND SPADES				
Bowl, 8"		$ 55.00	$ 75.00	
Plate, 7"		100.00	100.00	
Plate, 10"-12"		350.00		
WISTERIA				
Pitcher		$1,000.00	$1,750.00	
Tumbler		225.00	300.00	
WOODPECKER				
Wall pocket (vase)	$45.00			

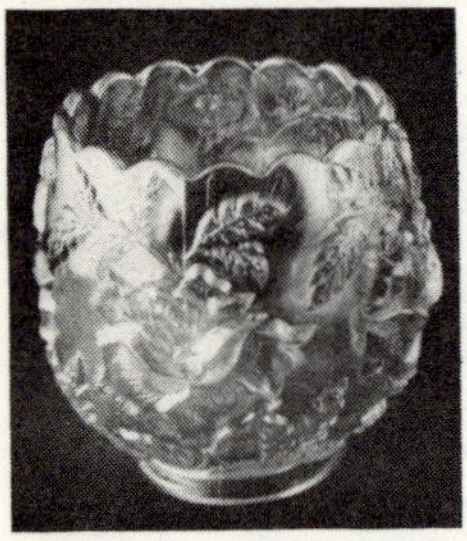

Pattern	Marigold	Green, Blue, Amethyst, Purple	Pastel	Red
WREATH OF ROSES				
Bonbon, footed	$ 40.00	$ 50.00		
Punch bowl with stand	175.00	250.00		
Punch cup	20.00	25.00		
Rose bowl	50.00	100.00		
ZIGZAG (decorated)				
Pitcher		$275.00		
Tumbler		70.00		
ZIGZAG (MILLERSBURG)				
Bowl, 8"-10"	$75.00	$125.00		

Pattern	Marigold	Green, Blue, Amethyst, Purple	Pastel	Red
ZIPPERED HEART				
Bowl, 9"	$ 50.00	$100.00		
Bowl, 5"	25.00	40.00		
Pitcher	350.00	700.00		
Tumbler	65.00	110.00		
Vase	950.00	950.00		
ZIPPERED LOOP				
Hand lamp	$250.00			
Sewing lamp, large	300.00			
Sewing lamp, small	300.00		$450.00	
AUSTRALIAN PATTERNS				
Australian swan bowl	$125.00	$175.00		
Emu bowl	125.00	175.00		
Kangaroo bowl	175.00	225.00		
Kingfisher	175.00	225.00		
Kiwi bowl	175.00	225.00		
Kookaburra bowl	175.00			
Magpie bowl	150.00			
Ostrich plate		300.00		
Thunderbird bowl	150.00	200.00		

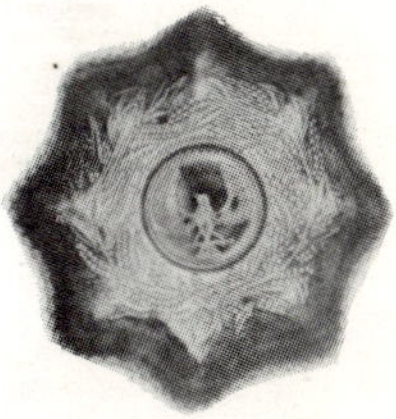